How the Poor Live

George R. Sims

Illustrated by Frederick Barnard

HOW THE POOR LIVE

BY GEORGE R. SIMS

WITH SIXTY ILLUSTRATIONS BY FREDERICK BARNARD

1883

PREFACE.

THE papers which form this volume appeared in the spring and summer of the present year in *The Pictorial World*. The interest now evinced in the great question of Housing the Poor leads me to hope that they will be of assistance to many who are studying the subject and, would desire to have their information in a convenient form for reference. Much that I ventured to prognosticate when "How the Poor Live" was written has happened since, and I have the permission of the author of "The Bitter Cry of Outcast London" to say that from these articles he derived the greatest assistance while compiling his now famous pamphlet. I have thought it well, all circumstances considered, to let the work stand in its original form, and have in no way added to it or altered it.

If an occasional lightness of treatment seems to the reader out of harmony with so grave a subject, I pray that he will remember the work was undertaken to enlist the sympathies of a class not generally given to the study of "low life."

I take this opportunity of expressing my gratitude to Mr. Frederick Barnard, the eminent artist, who, at considerable risk to his health and comfort, accompanied mc on a painful journey, and took his sketches "on the spot," amid the most distasteful surroundings.

GEORGE R. SIMS.

CHAPTER I.

COMMENCE with the first of this series of papers, a book of travel. An author and an artist have gone hand in hand into many a far-off region of the earth, and the result has been a volume eagerly studied by the stay-at-home public, anxious to know something of the world in which they live. In these pages I propose to record the results of a journey with pen and pencil into a region which lies at our own doors- into a dark continent that is within easy walking distance of the General Post Office. This continent will, I hope, be found as interesting as any of those newly-explored lands which engage the attention of the Royal Geographical Society - the wild races who inhabit will, I trust, gain public sympathy as easily as those savage tribes for whose benefit the Missionary Societies never cease to appeal for funds.

I have no shipwrecks, no battles, no moving adventures by flood and field to record. Such perils as I and my f ellow-traveller have encountered on our journey are not of the order which lend themselves to stirring narrative. It is unpleasant to be mistaken, in underground cellars where the vilest outcasts bide from the light of day, for detectives in search of their prey - it is dangerous to breathe for some hours at a stretch an atmosphere charged with infection and poisoned with indescribable effluvia - it is hazardous to be hemmed in down a blind alley by a crowd of roughs who have had hereditarily transmitted to them the maxim of John Leech, that half bricks were specially designed for the benefit of "strangers;" but these are not adventures of the heroic order, and they will not be dwelt upon lovingly after the manner of travellers who go farther afield.

My task is perhaps too serious a one even for the light tone of these remarks. No man who has seen " How the Poor Live" can return from the journey with aught but an aching heart. No man who recognises how serious is the social problem which lies before us, can approach its consideration in any but the gravest mood. Let me then briefly place before the reader the serious purpose of these papers, and then I will ask him to set out with me on the journey and judge for himself whether there is no remedy for much that he will see. He will have to encounter misery that some good people think it best to leave undiscovered. He will be brought face to face with that dark side of life which the wearers of rose-coloured spectacles turn away from on principle. The worship of the beautiful is an excellent thing, but he who digs down deep in the mire to find the soul of goodness in things evil, is a better man and a better Christian than he who shudders at the ugly and the unclean, and kicks it from his path, that it may not come between the wind and his nobility.

But let not the reader be alarmed, and imagine that I am about to take advantage of his good nature in order to plunge him neck high into a mud bath. He maybe pained before we part company, but he shall not be disgusted. He may occasionally feel a choking in his throat, but he shall smile now and again. Among the poor there is humour as well as pathos, there is food for laughter as well as for tears, and the rays of God's sunshine lose their way now and again, and bring light and gladness. into the vilest of the London slums.

His Royal Highness the Prince of Wales, in his speech at the opening of the Royal College of Music last May, said: "The time has come when class can no longer stand aloof from class, and that man does his duty best who works most earnestly in bridging over the gulf between different classes, which it is the tendency of increased wealth and increased civilisation to widen." It is to increased wealth and to increased civilisation that we owe the wide gulf which to-day separates well-to-do citizens from the masses. It is the increased wealth of this mighty city which has driven the poor back inch by inch, until we find them today herding together, packed like herrings in a barrel, neglected and despised, and left to endure wrongs and hardships which, if they were related to a far-off savage tribe, would cause Exeter Hall to shudder till its bricks fell down. It is the increased civilisation of this marvellous age which has made life a victory only for the strong, the gifted, and the specially blest, and left the weak, the poor, and the ignorant to work out in their proper persons the theory of the survival of the fittest to its bitter end.

There are not wanting signs that the "one-roomed helot" and his brood are about to receive a little scientific attention. They have become natural curiosities, and to this fact they may owe the honour in store for them, of dividing public attention with the Zenanas, the Aborigines, and the South Sea Islanders. The long-promised era of domestic legislation is said to be at hand, and prophets with powerful telescopes declare they can see the first faint signs of its dawn upon the political horizon. When that era has come within the range of the naked eye, it is probable that the Homes of the Poor will be one of its burning questions, and the strong arm of the law may be extended protectingly, even at the risk of showing the shortness of its sleeve, as far as the humble toilers who at the present moment suffer only its penalties and enjoy none of its advantages.

That there are remedies for the great evil which lies like a cankerworm in the heart of this fair city is certain. What those remedies are you will be better able to judge when you have seen the condition of the disease for which Dr. State is to be called in. Dr. State, alas, is as slow to put in an appearance as his parish *confrere* when the patient in need of his services is poor and friendless.

Forgive me this little discourse by the way. It has at any rate, filled up the time as we walk along to the outskirts of the land through which we are to travel for a few weeks together. And now, turning out of the busy street alive with the roar of commerce, and where the great mart and warehouses tower stories high, and where Dives adds daily to his wealth, we turn up a narrow court, and find ourselves at once in the slum where Lazarus lays his head - even as he did in the sacred story - at the very gates of the mighty millionaire.

We walk along a narrow dirty passage, which would effectually have stopped the Claimant had he come to this neighbourhood in search of witnesses, and at the end we find ourselves in what we should call a back yard, but which, in the language of the neighbourhood, is a square. The square is full of refuse, heaps of dust and decaying vegetable matter lie about here and there, under the windows and in front of the doors of the squalid tumble-down houses. The windows above and below are broken and patched, the roofs of these two-storied "eligible residences" look as thought Lord Alcester had been having some preliminary practice with his guns here before he set sail for Alexandria. All these places are let out in single rooms at prices varying from 2s. 6d. to 4s. a week. We can see a good deal of the inside through the cracks and crevices and broken panes, but if we knock at the door we shall get a view of the inhabitants.

If you knew more of these Alsatias, you would be rather astonished that there was a door to knock at. Most of the houses are open day and night, and knockers and bells are things unknown. Here, however, the former luxuries exist so we will not disdain them.

Knock, knock!

Hey presto! what a change of scene! Sleepy Hollow has come to life. Every door flies open, and there is a cluster of human beings on the threshold. Heads of matted hair and faces that haven't seen soap for months come out of the broken windows above.

Our knock has alarmed the neighbourhood. Who are we? The police? No. Who are we? Now they recognise one of our number - our guide - with a growl. He and we with him can pass without let or hindrance where it would be dangerous for a policeman to go. We are supposed to be on business connected with the School Board, and we are armed with a password which the worst of these outcasts have grown at last sulkily to acknowledge.

My fellow-traveller has sketched this result of a knock, we are not likely to see it again. This is a very respect- able place, and we have taken it first to break the ground gently for an artist who has not hitherto stu4ied "character" on ground where I have had many wanderings.

To the particular door attacked there comes a poor woman, white and thin, and sickly-looking; in her arms she carries a girl of eight or nine with a diseased spine; behind her, clutching at her scanty dress, are two or three other children. We put a statistical question, say a kind word to the little ones, and ask to see the room.

What a room! The poor woman apologises for its condition, but the helpless child, always needing her, and the other little ones to look after, and times being bad, &c. Poor creature, if she had ten pair of hands instead of one pair always full, she could not keep this room clean. The walls are damp and crumbling, the ceiling is black and peeling off, showing the laths above, the floor is rotten and broken away in places, and the wind and the rain sweep in through gaps that seem everywhere. The woman, her husband, and her six children live, eat, and sleep in this one room, and for this they pay three shillings a week. It is quite as much as they can afford. There has been no breakfast yet, and there won't be any till the husband (who has been out to try and get a job) conies in and reports progress. As to complaining of the dilapidated, filthy condition of the room, they know better. If they don't like it they can go. There are dozens of families who will jump at the accommodation, and the landlord is well aware of the fact.

Some landlords do repair their tenants' rooms. Why, cert'nly. Here is a sketch of one and of the repairs we saw the same day. Rent, 4s. a week; condition indescribable. But notice the repairs : a bit of a box lid nailed across a hole in the wall big enough for a man's head to go through, a nail knocked into a window frame beneath which still comes in a little fresh air, and a strip of new paper on a corner of the wall. You can't see the new paper because it is not up. The lady of the rooms holds it in her hand. The rent collector has just left it for her to put up herself. Its value, at a rough guess, is threepence. This landlord *has* executed repairs. Items: one piece of a broken soap-box. one yard and a-half of paper, and one nail. *And for these repairs he has raised the rent of the room threepence a week.*

We are not in the square now, but in a long dirty street, full of lodging-houses from end to end, a perfect human warren, where every door stands open night and day a state of things that shall be described and illustrated a little later on when we come to the "'appy dossers." In this street, close to the repaired residence, we select at hazard an open doorway and plunge into it. We pass along a greasy, grimy passage, and turn a corner to ascend the stairs. Round the corner it is dark. There is no staircase light, and we can hardly distinguish in the gloom where we are going. A stumble causes us to strike a light.

That stumble was a lucky one. Here is the staircase we were ascending, and which men and women and little children go up and down day after day, and night after night. The handrail is broken away, the stairs themselves are going - a heavy boot has been clean through one of them already, and it would need very little, one would think, for the whole lot to give way and fall with a crash. The sketch herewith, taken by the light of successive vestas, fail to give the grim horror of that awful staircase. The surroundings, the ruin, the decay, and the dirt, cannot be reproduced.

We are anxious to see what kind of people get safely up and down this staircase, and as we ascend them we knock accidentally up against something; it is a door and a landing. The door is opened, and as the light is thrown on to where we stand we give an involuntary exclamation of horror; the door opens right on to the corner stair. The woman who comes out would, if she stepped incautiously, fall six feet, and nothing could save her. It is a tidy room this, for the neighbourhood. A good hardworking woman has kept her home neat, even in such surroundings. The rent is four and sixpence a week, and the family living in it number eight souls; their total earnings are twelve shillings. A hard lot, one would fancy; but in comparison to what we have to encounter presently it certainly is . Asked about the stairs, the woman says, "It is a little ockard-like for the young'uns a-goin' up and down to school now the Board make 'em wear boots , but they don't often hurt themselves." Minus the boots, the children had got used to the ascent and descent, I suppose and were as much at home on the crazy staircase as a chamois on a precipice. *Excelsior* is our motto on this staircase. No maiden with blue eyes comes out to mention avalanches, but the woman herself suggests " it's werry bad higher up." We are as heedless of the warning as Longfellow's headstrong banner-bearer, for we go on.

It is "werry bad" higher up, so bad that we begin to light some more matches and look round to see how we are to get down. But as we continue to ascend the dark--ness gets less and less. We go a step at a time, slowly and circumspectly, up, up to the light, and at last our heads are suddenly above a floor and looking straight into a room.

We have reached the attic, and in that attic we see a picture which will be engraven on our memory for many a month to come.

The attic is almost bare; in a broken fireplace are some smouldering embers, a log of wood lies in front like a fen--der. There is a broken chair trying to steady itself against a wall black with the dirt of ages. In one corner, on a shelf, is a battered saucepan and a piece of dry bread. On the scrap of mantel still remaining embedded in the wall, is a rag; on a bit of cord hung across the room are more rags - garments of some sort, possibly ; a broken flower-pot props open a crazy window-frame, possibly to let the smoke out, or in - looking at the chimney-pots below, it is difficult to say which; and at one side of the room is a sack of Heaven knows what - it is a dirty, filthy sack, greasy and black and evil looking. I cannot guess what was in it if I tried, but what was on it was a little child - a neglected, ragged, grimed, and bare-legged little baby girl of four. There she sat, in the bare squalid room, perched on the sack, erect, motionless, expressionless, on duty.

She was "a little sentinel," left to guard a baby that lay asleep on the bare boards behind her, its head on its arm, the ragged remains of what had been a shawl flung over its legs.

That baby needed a sentinel to guard it, indeed. Had it crawled a foot or two it would have fallen head-foremost in that unprotected, yawning abyss of blackness below. In case of some such proceeding on its part, the child of four had been left "on guard."

The furniture of the attic, whatever it was like, had been seized the week before for rent. The little sentinel's papa - this we unearthed of the "deputy" of the house later on - as a militiaman and away; the little sentinel's mamma has gone out on " a arrand," which, if it was anything like her usual "arrands," the deputy below informed us, would bring her home about dark, very much the worse for it. Think of that little child, keeping guard on that dirty sack for six or eight hours at a stretch - think of her utter loneliness in that bare, desolate room, every childish impulse checked, left with orders "not to move or I'll kill yer," and sitting there often till night and darkness came on, hungry, thirsty, and tired herself but faithful to her trust to the last minute of the drunken mother's absence. "Bless yer! Ii've known that young 'un sit there eight 'our at a stretch. I've seen her there of a mornin' when I've come up to see if I could git the rint, and I've seen her there when I've come agin' at night" - says the deputy. "Lor, that ain't nothing - that ain't."

Nothing! It is one of the. saddest pictures I have seen for many a day. Poor little baby-sentinel - left with a human life in its sole charge at four - neglected and overlooked: what will its girl life be, when it grows old enough to think? 1 should like some of the little ones whose every wish is gratified, who have but to whimper to have, and who live surrounded by loving, smiling faces, and tendered by gentle hands, to see the little child in the bare garret sitting sentinel over the sleeping baby on the floor, and budging never an inch throughout the weary day from the place that her mother had bidden her stay in.

With our minds full of this pathetic picture of child-life in the "Homes of the Poor," we descend the crazy staircase, and get out into as much light as can find its way down these narrow alleys.

Outside we see a portly gentleman with a big gold chain across his capacious form, and an air of wealth and good living all over him. He is the owner of a whole block of property such as this, and he waxes rich on his rents. Strange as it may seem, these one-roomed outcasts are the across his capacious form, and an air of wealth and good living all over him. He is the owner of a whole block of property such as that, and he waxes rich on his rents. Strange as it may seem, these one-roomed outcasts are the best paying tenants in London. The pay so much for so little, and almost fight to get it. That they should be left to be thus exploited is a disgrace to the Legislature, which is never tired of protecting the oppressed of "all races that on earth do dwell," except those of that particular race who have the honour to be free-born Englishmen.

CHAPTER II.

A S I glance over the notes I have jotted down during my journey through outcasts' land, the delicacy of the task I have undertaken comes home to me more forcibly than ever. The housing of the poor and the remedy for the existing state of things are matters I have so much at heart that I fear lest I should not make ample use of the golden opportunities here afforded me of ventilating the subject. On the other hand, I hesitate to repel the reader, and, unfortunately, the best illustratons of the evils of overcrowding are repulsive to a degree.

Perhaps if I hint at a few of the very bad cases it will be sufficient. Men and women of the world will be able to supply the details and draw the correct deductions ; and it is, after all, only men and women of the world whose practical sympathy is likely to be enlisted by a revelation of the truth about the poor of great cities.

Come with me down this court, where at eleven o'clock in the morning a dead silence reigns. Every house is tenanted, but the blinds of the windows are down and the doors are shut. Blinds and doors! Yes, these luxuries are visible here. This is an aristocratic street, and the rents are paid regularly. There is no grinding poverty, no starvation here, and no large families to drag at the bread-winner. There is hardly any child-life here at all, for the men are thieves and highway cheats, and the women are of the class which has furnished the companions of such men from the earliest annals of roguedom.

The colony sleeps though the sun is high. The day with them is the idle time, and they reap their harvest in the hours of darkness. Later in the day, towards two o'clock, there will be signs of life ; oaths and shouts will issue from the now silent rooms, and there will be fierce wrangles and fights over the division of ill-gotten gains. The spirit of murder hovers over this spot, for life is held of little account. There is a Bill Sikes and Nancy in scores of these tenements, and the brutal blow is ever the accompaniment of the brutal oath.

These people, remember, rub elbows with the honest labouring poor; their lives are no mystery to the boys and girls in the neighbourhood ; the little girls often fetch Nancy's gin, and stand in a gaping crowd while Nancy and Bill exchange compliments on the doorstep, drawn from the well of Saxon, impure and utterly defiled. The little boys look up half with awe and half with admiration at the burly Sikes with his flash style, and delight in gossip concerning his talents as a "cribcracker", and his adventures as a pickpocket. The poor-the honest poor-have been driven by the working of the Artizans' Dwellings Acts, and the clearance of rookery after rookery, to come and herd with thieves and wantons, to bring up their children in the last Alsatias, where lawlessness and violence still reign supreme.

The constant association of the poor and the criminal class has deadened in the former nearly all sense of right and wrong. In the words of one of them, "they can't afford to be particular about their choice of neighbours." I was but the other day in a room in this district occupied by a widow woman, her daughters of seventeen and sixteen, her sons of fourteen and thirteen, and two younger children Her wretched apartment was on the street level, and behind it was the common yard of the tenement. In this yard the previous night a drunken sailor had been desperately maltreated and left for dead. I asked the woman if she had not heard the noise, and why she didn't interfere. "Heard it?" was the reply; "well, we ain't deaf, but they're a rum lot in this here house, and we're used to rows. There ain't a night passes as there ain't a fight in the passage or a drunken row; but why should I interfere? Tain't no business of mine." As a matter of fact, this woman, her grown-up daughters, and her boys must have lain in that room night after night, hearing the most obscene language, having a perfect knowledge of the proceedings of the vilest and most depraved of profligate men and women forced upon them, hearing cries of murder and the sound of blows, knowing that almost every crime in the Decalogue was being committed in that awful back yard on which that broken casement looked, and yet not one of them had ever dreamed of stirring hand or foot. They. were saturated with the spirit of the place, and though they were respectable people themselves they saw nothing criminal in the behaviour of their neighbours.

For this room, with its advantages, the widow paid four and sixpence a week; the walls were mildewed and streaming with damp, the boards as you trod upon them made the slushing noise of a plank spread across a mud puddle in a brickfield: foul within and foul without, these people paid the rent of it gladly. and perhaps thanked God for the luck of having it. Rooms for the poor earning precarious livelihoods are too hard to get and too much in demand now for a widow woman to give up one just because of the trifling inconvenience of overhearing a few outrages and murders.

One word more on this shady subject and we will get out into the light again. I have spoken of the familiarity of the children of the poor with all manners of wickedness and crime. Of all the evils arising from this one-room system there is perhaps none greater than the utter destruction of innocence in the young. A moment's thought will enable the reader to appreciate the evils of it. But if it is had in the case of a respectable family, how much more terrible is it when the children are familiarised with actual immorality.

Wait outside while we knock at this door.

Knock, knock.-No answer!

Knock, knock, knock!

A child's voice answers, " What is it?"

We give the answer - the answer which has been our "open, sesame" everywhere-and after a pause a woman opens a door a little and asks us to wait a moment. Presently we are admitted. A woman pleasing looking and with a certain refinement in her features holds the door open for us. She has evidently made a hurried toilet and put on an ulster over her night attire. She has also put a brass chain and locket round her neck. There is a little rouge left on her cheeks and a little of the burnt hairpin colour left under her eyes from overnight. At the table having their breakfast are two neat and clean little girls of seven and eight.

MOTHER AND DAUGHTERS.

They rise and curtsey as we enter. We ask them a few question, and they answer intelligently - they are at the Board School and are making admirable progress - charming children, interesting and well-behaved in every way. They have a perfect knowledge of good and evil - one of them has taken a Scripture prize - and yet these two charming and intelligent little girls live in that room night and day with their mother, and this is the den to which she snares her dissolute prey.

I would gladly have passed over this scene in silence, but it is one part of the question which directly bears on the theory of State interference. It is by shutting our eyes to evils that we allow them to continue unreformed so long. I maintain that such cases as these are fit ones for legislative protection. The State should have the power of rescuing its future citizens from such surroundings, and the law which protects young children from physical hurt should also be so framed as to shield them from moral destruction.

The worst effect of the present system of Packing the Poor is the moral destruction of the next generation. Whatever it costs us to remedy the disease we shall gain in decreased crime and wickedness. It is better even that the ratepayers should bear a portion of the burthen of new homes for the respectable poor than that they should have to pay twice as much in the long run for Prisons, Lunatic Asylums, and Workhouses.

Enough for the present of the criminal classes. Let us see some of the poor people who earn an honest living - well, "living " perhaps, is hardly the word - let us say, who can earn enough to pay their rent and keep body and soul together.

Here is a quaint scene, to begin with. When we open the door we start back half choked. The air is full of floating fluff, and some of it gets into our months and half chokes us. When we've coughed and *wheezed* a little we look about us and gradually take in the situation.

"RABBIT-PULLING."

The room is about eight feet square. Seated on the floor is a white fairy - a dark-eyed girl who looks as though she had stepped straight off a twelfth cake. Her hair is pow- dered all over *a la Pompadour,* and the effect is *bizarre.* Seated beside her is an older woman, and she is white and twelfth-cakey too. Alas, their occupation is prosaic to a degree. They are simply pulling rabbit-skins - that is to say they are pulling away all the loose fluff and down and preparing the skins for the furriers, who will use them for cheap goods, dye them into imitations of rarer skins, and practise upon them the various tricks of the trade.

Floor, walls, ceiling, every inch of the one room these people live and sleep in, is covered with fluff and hair. How they breathe in it is a mystery to me. I tried and failed, and sought refuge on the doorstep. The pair, working night and day at their trade, make, when business is good, about twelve shillings a week. Their rent is four. This leaves them four shillings a week each to live upon, and as there is no one else to share it with them, I suppose they are well-to-do folk.

The younger woman s appearance was striking. Seated on the floor in an Eastern attitude, and white from top to toe-the effect of her dark eyes heightened by the contrast - she was a picture for an artist, and my fellow-worker made excellent use of his pencil, while I engaged her and her mother in conversation.

These people complained bitterly of their. surroundings, of the character of the people they had to live among, and of the summary proceedings of their landlord, who absolutely refused to repair their room or give them the slightest convenience.

"Then why not move?" I ventured to suggest. "Four shillings a week - ten guineas a year for this pigstye - is an exorbitant rent - you might do better."

The woman shook her head. "There's lots o' better places we'd like to go to, but they won't have us. They object to our business. We must go where they'll take us."

"But there are plenty of places a little way out where you can have two rooms for what you pay for this."

"A little way out, yes; but how are we to get to and fro with the work when it's done? We must be near our work. We can't afford to ride."

Exactly! And therein lies one of the things which reformers have to consider. There are thousands of these families who would go away into the suburbs, where we want to get them, if only the difficulty of travelling expenses to and from could be conquered. They herd together all in closely packed quarters because they must be where they can get to the dock, the yard, the wharf, and the warehouses without expense. The highest earnings of this class is rarely above sixteen shillings a week, and that, with four or five shillings for rent, leaves very little margin where the family is large. The omnibus and the train are the magicians which will eventually hid the rookeries disappear, but the services of these magicians cost money, and there is none to spare in the pockets of the poor.

A PROTESTANT DARRIE.

In another room close to these people, but if anything in a more wretched condition still, we come upon a black man sitting with his head buried in his hands. He is suffering with rheumatics, and has almost lost the use of his limbs.

The reason is evident. His wife points to the bed in the corner against the wall, the damp is absolutely oozing through and trickling down the wall. The black man is loquacious. He is a hawker, and can't go out and lay in a stock, for he hasn't a penny in the world. He is stone broke. He is a Protestant darkie, he informs us, and is full of troubles. Two boys are lolling about on the floor. At our entrance a shock-headed ragged girl of ten has crawled under the bed. The Protestant darkie drags her out and explains she is "a-bringin' him to his grave with sorrer- she's a bad gel and slangs her mother". The P. D. doesn't know how he's going to pay his rent or where the next meal's coming from. He stands outside "a corffee shop" generally, when he can get about, and the lady as keeps it, bless her - she's a rare good on to me - she's a fallen angel, that's what she is " but he can't go and hawk nothing, else he'd be took up. "I ain't got no capital, and, faith of a Protestant darkie, I'm defunct."

The man has a host of quaint sayings and plenty of the peculiar wit of the nigger breed, but his position is undoubtedly desperate.

The rent of the death-trap he lives in with his wife and family is four and sixpence, and his sole means of subsistence is hawking shrimps and winkles when they are cheap, or specked oranges and damaged fruit. He has at the best of times only a shilling or two to lay out in the wholesale market, and out of his profit he must pay his rent and keep his family. I suspect that the "fallen angel" is often good for a meal to the poor darkie, and I learn that he is a most respectable, hardworking fellow "How do you do when you're stone broke?" I ask him. "Well, sir, sometimes I comes across a gentleman as gives me a bob and starts me again."

The shot hits the mark, and we leave the Protestant darkie grinning at his own success, and debating with his wife what will be the best article in which to invest for the day's market.

Honest folks enough in their way, these,-keeping themselves to themselves and struggling on as best they can, now "making a bit over," and now wondering where on earth the next sixpence is to come from. Just up the street is a house with an inscription over it which tells us we can find within a very different class to study. This is a licensed lodging-house, where you can be accommodated for 4d. or 6d. a night. This payment gives you during the day the privilege of using the common kitchen, and it is into the common kitchen we are going. We walk into the passage, and are stopped by a strapping young woman of about eight and twenty. She is the deputy. "What do we want ?"

Once again the password is given, and the attitude of the lady changes. She formally conducts us into a large room, where the strangest collection of human beings are crowded together. It is sheet-washing day, and there is a great fire roaring up the chimney. Its ruddy glare gives a Rembrandtisb tone to the picture. Tables and forms run round the room, and there is not a vacant place. Men, women, and children are lolling about, though it is midday, apparently with nothing to do but make themselves comfortable. The company is not a pleasant one. Many of the men and women and boy are thieves. Almost every form of disease, almost every kind of deformity, seems crowded into this Chamber of Horrors. The features are mostly repulsive an attractive face there is not among the sixty or seventy human beings in the room. Some of them are tramps and hawkers, but most of them are professional loafers, picking up in any way that presents itself the price of a night's lodging. They are a shifting population, and rarely remain in one house long. Some of them only get a night in now and then as a luxury, and look upon it as a Grand Hotel episode. They sheep habitually in the open, on the staircases, or in the casual ward. The house we are in is one where Nancy and Sikes come often enough when they are down on their luck. Here is a true story of this very place, which will perhaps illustrate sufficiently the type of its frequenters.

Some time last year two men left the house one morning. They were going into the country on business. One, whom I will call John, kissed his mistress, a girl of twenty, and said "Good-bye," leaving her at the house; he wouldn't be away long, and he and Bill, his companion, set out on their travels.

A day or two after Bill returns alone, the girl asks him where her sweetheart is. "He's lagged," says Bill. But the girl has a bit of newspaper, and in it she reads that "the body of a man has been found in some woods near London; and she has an idea it may be John. "Oh, nonsense," says Bill-I quote the evidence- "he then lit his candle, and they retired to rest." John, as a matter of fact, had been murdered by his companion, they having quarrelled over the division of the proceeds of the burglary; and eventually this young woman, who so readily transferred her affections from one lord to another, appeared in the witness-box and deposed to pawning boots and other things for Bill which were undoubtedly the proceeds of a robbery at a house chose to where the body was found.

This is the house in which we stand where the burglary was planned whence the murderer and the murdered set out together on their fatal journey. It was at one of these tables that the young girl discussed her absent lover's fate with her new lord his murderer, and it was here that the police came to search for him and found the girl whose evidence helped to hang him.

Look at the people who sit there to-day - murderers and burglars some of them, cheats and pickpockets others, and a few respectable folks as far as their opportunities will allow. But remember that dozens of really respectable families who have to frequent these places nosy, and mix with malefactors day and night, because there are no other places open to them.

Among all the cruelties practised on the poor in the name of Metropolitan Improvements this one deserves mentioning - that the labourer earning a precarious livelihood with his wife and his children have been driven at last to accept the shelter of a thieves' kitchen and to be thankful for it.

CHAPTER III

I CANNOT help being struck, in my wanderings through Povertyopolis, with the extraordinary resemblance which Caesar bore to Pompey - especially Pompey. One room in this district is very like the other. The family likeness of the chairs and tables is truly remarkable, especially in the matter of legs. Most chairs are born with four legs, but the chairs one meets with here are a two-legged race - a four-legged chair is a *rara avis,* and when found should be made a note of. The tables, too, are of a type indigenous to the spot. The survival of the fittest does not obtain in these districts in the matter of tables. The most positively unfit are common, very common objects. What has become of the fittest I hesitate to conjecture. Possibly they have run away. I am quite sure that a table with legs would make use of them to escape from such surroundings.

A FURNISHED APARTMENT.

As to the bedsteads. they are wretched, broken-down old things of wood and iron that look as though they had been rescued a little late from a fire, then used for a barricade, afterwards buried in volcanic eruption, and finally dug out of a dust-heap that had concealed them for a century. The bedding, a respectable coal-sack would blush to acknowledge even as a poor relation.

I have enumerated chairs, tables, and beds-not because they are found in every poor home ; there are several rented rooms which can boast of nothing but four walls, a ceiling, and a floor, but because these articles placed in one of these dens constitute what are euphemistically called "furnished apartments," a species of accommodation with which all very poor neighbourhoods abound.

The " furnished apartments" fetch as much as tenpence a day, and are sometimes occupied by three or four different tenants during a week.

The "deputy" comes for the money every day, and it is pay or go with the occupants. If the man who has taken one of these furnished rooms for his "home, sweet home," does not get enough during the day to pay his rent, out he goes into the street with his wife and children, and enter another family forthwith.

The tenants have not, as a rule, much to be flung after them in the shape of goods and chattels. The clothes they stand upright in, a battered kettle and, perhaps, a bundle, make up the catalogue of their worldly possessions.

This rough-and-ready lodging is the resource of thousands of industrious people earning precarious livelihoods, and they rarely rise above it to the dignity of taking a room by the week. The great struggle is to get over Saturday, and thank God for Sunday. Sunday is a free day, and no deputy comes to disturb its peaceful calm. The Saturday's rent, according to the custom of the country, makes the tenant free of the apartments until Monday.

It is the custom to denounce the poor as thriftless, and that they are so I grant. The temptation to trust to luck and let every day take care of itself is, it must be remembered, great. Life with them is always a toss-up, a daily battle, an hourly struggle. Thousands of them can never hope to be five shillings ahead of the world if they keep honest. The utmost limit of their wage is reached when they have paid the rent, kept themselves and their horribly large families from starvation, and bought the few rags which keep their limbs decently covered. With them the object of life is attained when the night's rent is paid, and they do not have to hesitate between the workhouse or a corner of the staircase in some doorless house.

There is a legend in one street I know of - a man who once saved half-a-crown, and lost it through a hole in his pocket. The moral of that legend may have improved itself upon the whole population and discouraged thrift for evermore; but be that as it may, the general rule is, "what you make in a day, spend in a day." It is needless to add that this precept brings its practisers perpetually within measureable distance of absolute penniless. They live and die on the confines of it. I am wrong; they invariably die on the wrong side of the border, and are buried at somebody else's expense.

Drink is the curse of these communities; but how is it to be wondered at? The gin-palaces flourish in the slums, and fortunes are made out of men and women who seldom know where to-morrow's meal is coming from.

Can you wonder that the gaudy gin-palaces, with their light and their glitter, are crowded? Drink is sustenance to these people ; drink gives them the Dutch courage necessary to go on living ; drinks dulls their senses and reduces them to the level of the brutes they must be to live in such styes.

The gin-palace is Heaven to them compared to the Hell of their pestilent homes. A copper or two often obtained by pawning the last rag that covers the shivering children on the bare floor at house will buy enough vitriol madness to send a woman home so besotted that the wretchedness, the anguish, the degradation that await her there have lost their grip. To be drunk with these people means to be happy. Sober - God help them! - how could they be aught but wretched.

There is not only temptation to drink wrought by the fearful surroundings of the poor; a positive craving for it is engendered by the foul and fetid atmosphere they continually breathe. I have often wondered that the advocates of temperance, with the immense resources of wealth and organisations they command, have not given more attention to the overcrowding and the unsanitary condition of the dwellings of the poor, as one of the great causes of the abuse of stimulants.

It is not only that crime and vice and disorder flourish luxuriantly in these colonies, through the dirt and discomfort bred of intemperance of the inhabitants, but the effect upon the children is terrible. The offspring of drunken fathers and mothers inherit not only a tendency to vice, but they come into the world physically and mentally unfit to conquer in life's battle. The wretched, stunted, mis-shapen child-object one comes upon in these localities, is the most painful part of our explorers' experience. The county asylums are crowded with pauper idiots and lunatics, who owe their wretched condition to the sin of the parents, and the rates are heavily burthened with the maintenance of the idiot offspring of drunkenness.

The drink dulls every sense of shame, takes the sharp edge from sorrow, and leaves the drinker for a while in a fool's paradise. Here is the home of the most notorious "drunkardess"- if I may coin a word - in the neighbourhood. Mrs. O'Flannigan's room is easily entered, for it is on the street level, and one step brings us into the presence of the lady herself. She is in bed, a dirty red flannel rag is wrapped about her shoulders, and her one arm is in a sling. She sits up in bed at the sight of visitors, and greets us in a gin and fog voice slightly mellowed with the Irish brogue. Biddy has been charged at the police-courts seventy-five times with being drunk, and she is therefore a celebrated character. She is hardly sober now, though she has evidently had a shaking which would have sobered most people for a month. Her face is a mass of bruises and cuts, and every now and then a groan and a cry to certain Saints in her calendar tell of aches and pains in the limbs concealed under the dirty blanket that covers the bed.

"I'm a pretty sight now, ain't I, gintlemen dear?" she says, with a foolish laughs. " Shure and I got blind drunk again last Saturday, and they run me in. The inspector let me out o' Sunday: God bless him for a rale gintleman. They carried me on a stretcher, bless yer hearts, and I kicked. Ha! ha! ha! " The hag positively yelled with laughter as she thought of the scene she caused and the trouble she gave the police.

Suddenly she looks round as if in search of something.

"Molly, ye young varmint, where are ye?" she shouts, and presently, from under the bed, where it lay crouching in fear, she drags a child, a wretched little girl of seven or eight, with its face and head a covered with sores, that make one shudder to look at them.

"There, Molly, ye young varmint, show yourself to their honours, will ye?"

The child begins to snivel. One of our number is the Board School officer of the district, and Molly has not been to school lately. Mrs. O'Flannigan explains.

"Ye see,. I can't use my limbs just yet, yer honour, and Molly - Lord love her! - she's just the only thing I got to look afther me. I might be burned in my blessed bed, yer honour and not able to move."

"You should give up getting drunk," I ventured to suggest; "then you wouldn't want a nurse."

"You're right, your honour. It's the drink. Yer see, I can't help it. I ain't been sober for five years - ha! ha! ha! - and it's all thro' the trouble as come to me. My boy got into bad company and got lagged and put away for ten years, and I've never been the same since, and it broke nay heart, and I took to the drink. And now my old man's took to drink thro' aggravation o' me, and he gets drunk every night of his blessed life. Ha! ha! ha!"

MRS. O'FLANNIGAN.

The woman's story is practically true. Before her trouble she and her husband were costermongers and hawkers of fruit. The first of the evils of the foul slums where honest workers are forced to live, fell upon them in the ruin of the boy reared in a criminal atmosphere. The vicious surroundings were too strong for him, and he became a thief and paid the penalty.

The mother sees her son - idolised in her rough way - taken from her; the den of a home becomes doubly wretched, and the cursed drink-fiend is invoked to charm the sorrow away. That is the first step "to drown sorrow." The steps after that are easy to count. The woman becomes an habitual drunkard, the rooms they live in get dirtier and smaller and fouler, and at last the husband drowns his sorrow too. "Aggravation" and a constant association with a drunken woman turn the poor fellow to evil ways himself and a whole family are wrecked, that under better circumstances might have been good and useful citizens. Had these people been able to get a decent room among decent people, the first misfortune that sent them wrong might never have happened. Their case is the case of hundreds.

Of drinking-shops there are plenty in these places ; of eating-houses, or shops for the sale of food, very few. So rare are the latter that when we come to one in a dirty, tumble-down street, we stop and examine the contents of the window. I don't know whether to call it a tart-shop, a baker's, or a dripping emporium. There seems to be a little bit of each about it, and half a rice-pudding, and a ham-bone, on which a bluebottle has gone to sleep - tired out perhaps with looking for the meat - give it the faintest suspicion of being an eating-house. There is also in the window a dilapidated bloater which looks as though it had been ruts over by an omnibus many years ago.

It is while taking notes of the contents of this tempting emporium of luxuries that we become aware of a very powerful perfume. It seems to rise from beneath where we are standing, and used as we are by this time to the bouquets of the east, we involuntarily step back and contort the muscles of our faces.

Then we see that we have been standing on a grating. Peering down we can just see into a gloomy little room. To the opened window presently there comes a man in his shirt-sleeves and looks up at us. His face is deadly white, the eyes are sunken, the cheek bones hollow, and there is a look in his face that says more plainly than the big ticket of the blind impostor, "I am starving." Starving down below there, with only a thin floor between himself and the ham-bone, the ancient herring, the rice pudding, and the treacle tarts.

As the noisome effluvia rises and steams through the grating we begin to appreciate the situation. This food shop is directly over the cellar which gives the odour forth. Pleasant for the customers, certainly. We determine to push our investigation still further, and presently we down in the cellar below.

THE TART SHOP.

The man in his shirt-sleeves - we can guess where coat is - receives us courteously. His wife apologises the wretched condition of the room. Both of them speak with that unmistakable *timbre* of voice which betokens a smattering of education. In the corner of the room is a heap of rags. That is the bed. There are two children, a boy and a girl, sitting on a bare hearth and gazing into the fast dying embers of a wretched fire. Furniture the room has absolutely none, but a stool roughly constructed of three pieces of unplaned wood nailed together.

THE OCCUPANT OF THE CELLAR.

Four shillings a week is the rent of the cellar below the pie-shop - the foul smell arises from the gradual decay of the basement and the utter neglect of all sanitary precautions.

The man (who has only one arm) is out of work this week, he tells us, but he is promised a job next. To tide over till then is a work of some difficulty, but the "sticks" and the "wardrobe" of the family have paid the rent up to now. As to meals - well, they hain't got much appetite. The stench in which they live effectually destroys that. In this instance even bad drainage has its advantages, you see.

Before the man lost his arm he was a clerk; without a right hand he is not much good as a penman in a competitive market. So he goes on as timekeeper in a builder's yard, as a messenger, or as anything he can get a few shillings at for a living.

The children have not been to school. "Why?" asks the officer who accompanies us. "Because they've no boots, and they are both ill now." It is true. The children, pale, emaciated little things, cough a hard rasping cough from time to time. To show us how bad they are they set up a perfect paroxysm of coughing until the mother fetches them a smack, and inquires "how they expect the gentleman to hear himself speak if they kick up *that* row?"

The children's boots have gone with the father's coat, and at present it does seem hard to say that the parents must be fined unless the children come barefooted through the sloppy streets to school.

Such, however, is the rule, and this boot question is an all-important one in the compulsory education of the children of the slums. How to get the boots for Tommy and Sarah to go their daily journey to the Board School problem which one or two unhappy fathers have settled by hanging themselves behind the domestic door.

The difficulties which the poor have in complying with the demands of the Education Act are quite unsuspected by the general public. They are so numerous, and the histories revealed by their investigation are so strange, that I propose in the next Chapter to ask the reader to accompany me to a meeting at which the parental excuses for non- attendance are made. This is a meeting at which the parents who have been summoned for the non-attendance of their children adduce what reasons they can why they should not be summoned before a magistrate.

I will let the mothers and fathers tell their own tale, and give a few statistics which I fancy will be revelation to many who are at present in sublime ignorance of

"HOW THE POOR LIVE."

CHAPTER IV.

IN the remote age when I was a good little boy I remember being induced to join a Dorcas meeting. Don't imagine that I ever so far forgot the dignity of my sex as to sew or make little flannel petticoats and baby-linen for the poor of the parish. The young ladies did that, and we - myself and about ten other good little boys - were inveigled into joining on the plea, that while our sisters plied needle and thread we could stick scraps into books and colour them, make toys, and perform various other little feats of usefulness which would eventually benefit the benighted Hottentots.

I know that when I had consented to join I was in agonies till the first day of meeting arrived, and wondered to what I had committed myself; and I remember to this day how very red I blushed when I arrived late and found fifty other good little boys and girls assembled, all of whom looked up and eyed me as though I was a natural curiosity, when the good lady who directed the society said, "This is little Master So-and-so, who has come to help us in our good work."

How I got past all those little girls I don't know, but I kept my eyes fixed modestly on the ground, and at last found myself seated at a table with about a dozen young gentlemen of my own age.

The elderly, good-hearted spinster who presided instantly deposited in front of me a huge l)ot of paste, an empty book, and some old illustrated papers. I guessed what she intended me to do, and I made wild efforts to do it. I was informed that this book, when I had completed it, would be sold at a bazaar for the benefit of the Heathen.

I never ascertained what that book did fetch, but I know that it never paid expenses. The mess that I got into with that paste, the way it would get all over my fingers, and onto my coat-sleeve, and all down me and all over me - why, I wrecked a whole suit, which in my vanity I put on new, at a single sitting. That was my first introdn for; to scissors and paste, and I took an intense dislike to them.

I quote the reminiscence because this article is to be all about a "B" meeting; and when I first heard of a "B" meeting I made sure it must be something like a Dorcas meeting, where everybody was a busy bee, and did work for the poor.

I had not had a very long experience before I found out that it was something not half as pleasant as the scrap-book and flannel petticoat society of my youth.

A "B" meeting is held under the auspices of the School Board, to hear the reasons parents may have to give why they should not be summoned to appear before a magistrate for neglecting to send their children to school.

Here is an exact reproduction of the Notice B left with the parents, which brings them to the meeting I am about to describe, and my collaborator to illustrate.

[Bye-laws] [Form No.13]

NOTICE - FORM B.

The Elementary Education Acts, 1870, 1873, and 1876.

SCHOOL BOARD FOR LONDON.

Notice to attend before Divisional Committee.

.... Division.

May 30, 1883.

To Mr. Bridge, 2, Smith's Court.

Take Notice, that you have been guilty of a breech of the of the law in that your child Robert has not duly attended school, and you are hereby invited to attend at George Street School on Wednesday, the 6th day of June, at 2 o'clock in the afternoon precisely, to state any excuse you may have, and to show cause why you should not be summoned before a magistrate and fined.

Dated this 31st day of May, 1883.

(Signed) ....

Officer of the School Board for London.

(SEAL)

Few persons who have not actual experience of the lives of the poorest classes can have any conception of the serious import to them of the Education Act. Compulsory education is a national benefit. I am one of its stoutest defenders, but it is idle to deny that it is an Act which has gravely increased the burthens of the poor earning precarious livelihoods and as self-preservation is the first law of nature, there is small wonder that every dodge that craft and cunning can suggest is practised to evade it.

In many cases the payment of the fees is a most serious difficulty. Twopence or a penny a week for each of four children is not much, you may say; but where the difference between the weekly income and the rent is only a couple of shillings or so, I assure you the coppers represent so many meals. The Board now allows the members to remit fees in cases of absolute inability to pay them, and the remission of fees is one of the principal items of business at a "B" meeting.

Again, many of the children who are of school age are of a wage-earning age also, and their enforced "idleness", as their parents call it, means a very serious blow to the family exchequer. Many a lad whose thick skull keeps him from passing the standard which would leave him free to go to work, has a deft hand, strong arms and a broad back - three things which fetch a fair price in the labour market. As I will show you presently, from the actual cases which come before the "B" meeting, the hardship of making boys and girls stop at school who might be earning good money towards their support, is terrible. Often these children are the *sole* bread-winners, and then the position is indeed a hard nut for the kind-hearted official to crack.

After the children have passed a certain standard the officials have the power of granting "half-time"; that is to say, the boys and girls can earn money so many days a week, and come to school for the remainder. "The half-time grant" is another feature of the "B" meeting.

The worst duty of the official who presides is to authorise the summoning before a magistrate of the parents who cannot or will not send their children regularly. The law leaves him no option. All children must come unless illness or some equally potent excuse can be urged, and if they don't the parent must appear before a magistrate, who, if the case is made out, is bound by the law to impose a fine. I will endeavour to show you, as the meeting progresses, a few of the parents who thoroughly deserve the penalty.

A "B" meeting is held in the up-stairs room of one of the Board Schools. Here is a sketch of one in full swing. The summoned parents are waiting in a huge crowd outside. They come in one by one to be disposed of. You will easily recognise the president of the meeting, with the book before him, in which the cases to be heard are fully entered up. Beside him sits the Board official, the inspector of officers, who advises him on little points of School Board law, and who marks the papers which are to be returned to the School Board officer "in charge of the case" to be acted upon.

The gentlemen standing round the room are the School Board officers of the different divisions in the district. They are familiar with the history and circumstances of every one who will come into the little room, and they will supply confirmation or contradiction as the necessity arises.

Somewhere or other in the scene the artist has, I perceive, depicted "us." Where, I leave the reader to discover. We are accepted by the parents who come and go as part and parcel of the "Inquisition," and some care is necessary in executing our task, for this class is very great on the rights of property; and more than one energetic dame, if she knew her face was being "scratched" by an unauthorised interloper, would literally return the compliment.

"The short and simple annals of the poor," here related in their own words, will induct the reader into the mysteries of "How they live" far more thoroughly than I could do did I fill pages with my own composition; so, silence, pray, and let the "B" meeting commence.

Here is a lady who very much objects to being summoned.

"What bizerness 'as he to summings me," she says, pointing to the officer, "just cus my boy ain't bin fur a week? He's 'arsh and harbitury, that's what he is. 'Arsh and harbitury. D'ye think I ain't got anything to do without a-trapesin' down here a-losin' my work. I tell ye what it is-"

The chairman mildly interposes- "My good lady-"

"Don't good lady me. I ain't a lady. If I was you daren't treat me like it, you daren't ; it's only because I'm-"

"My good woman, will you allow me to say one word?"

"Oh-yes-certainly-if you've got anything to say- go on."

Thus encouraged the chairman points out to the voluble lady that her son has not been to school for a fortnight.

"Well, it's all through the boots."

"Boots! " says the chairman; "why, that was what you said last time, and we gave you an order on a shoemaker for a pair."

The woman acknowledges this is so. Some charitable people have started a fund to let a few bad cases have boots and this truant has been one of the first recipients.

"I know you was kind enough to do that," says the mother, "but they 'urt him and he can't wear 'em."

"HE'S 'ARSH AND HARDITURY, THAT'S WHAT HE IS, 'ARSH AND HARDITURY."

Here the officer who has brought the lady up before the Board tells *his* story.

"The boy had a decent pair of boots supplied him, sir; but Mrs. Dash went back to the shop with him, and said they weren't good enough - she wanted a pair of the best the man had in stock, and made such a noise she had to be put out."

"Which, beggin' your pardon," strikes in the angry lady, "it's like your imperence to say so. They 'urt the boy, they did, and he haves tender feet, through his father, as is dead, being a shoemaker hisself."

The officer chimes in again, "If he can play about the streets all day in the boots, Mrs. Dash, they can't hurt him very much."

"My boy play about the streets! Well, of all the oudacious things as ever I 'erd! And as to his comin' to school he's a beautiful little scholard now, and he ain't got no more to learn."

Eventually the "beautiful little scholard," who was waiting outside, was sent for. Here he is.

"A BEAUTIFUL LITTLE SCHOLARD."

He confessed that the boots didn't hurt him, and Mrs. Dash was informed that if he didn't forthwith attend she would be summoned.

With much difficulty Mrs. Dash was induced to retire, and her place was taken by a burly man covered with grime from a forge, or something of the sort, who hooked the personification of fierceness and stoney-heartedness. His daughter had not been to school lately, and he was asked to account for her absence.

"I'M VERY SORRY, SIR, BUT I'VE HAD A LITTLE TROUBLE."

There was a moment's pause. We expected an oath, or a volley of abuse. Instead of that the man's lips trembled a moment, then his eyes filled with tears, and one rolled slowly down each grimy cheek.

In a choking voice he gasped out, "I am very sorry, sir, but I've had a little trouble."

"Dear me!" says the chairman, slightly staggered at the unusual display of emotion ; "I am sorry for that. What sort of trouble ?"

"Well, sir, it ain't a pleasant thing to talk about, -sob- but my wife, -sob- she's left me, sir, -sob-" gone away with another man."

Here the poor fellow broke down utterly and sobbed like a child. Then he drew a dirty rag from his pocket, and rubbed and rubbed it round his eyes till there was a white ring about them that looked like a pair of spectacles.

The effect was ludicrous, but no one smiled. The audience, as they say in theatrical notices, was visibly affected.

The man stammered out his tale bit by bit. His wife had left him with four little children. He had to go out to work, and his daughter he had to keep away from school to look after them. She had to be "little mother " in the deserted home.

I wondered what the woman was like, and if she had any idea of the genuine love for her that welled up in this honest fellow's heart. As I watched the tears flow down his grimy face, I couldn't help thinking how many a noble dame would like to know that her absence from the domestic hearth would cause grief as genuine as this.

Under the painful circumstances the excuse was accepted; the "little mother" was allowed a short holiday till the betrayed husband had time to make other arrangements, and he left the room murmuring his thanks and mopping his eyes.

"Mrs. Smith," calls out the Board official, taking the next case down on the list for hearing, and a young girl of about fifteen, with a baby in her arms and a child of five clinging to her skirts, enters the room and seats herself nervously on the extreme edge of the chair.

"You're not Mrs. Smith, my dear," says the chairman, with a smile.

"No, sir; that's mother."

"Oh, you've come for her, eh? These boys, Thomas and Charles, who have been absent for three weeks, are your brothers, I suppose?"

"Yes, sir."

"Well, my dear, they ought to come, you know. What's the reason?"

"Please, sir, they're at work."

"But they've not passed the Fourth Standard."

"I know, sir; but they've got a job, and it's four shillings week each, and that's all I've got to keep us."

"All *you've* got, my dear? Where's your father?"

The girl colours a little and hesitates. The School Board officer steps forward to the table and helps her.

"It's a very painful case, sir," he says. "The father's been living with another woman - left his family. A fortnight ago the mother met him and asked him for some money. He knocked her down, and she fell and cut her head open. She's in St. Thomas's Hospital - not expected to live. The man was taken up, and he's under remand now, and this girl has to look after the entire family."

"I see," says the chairman ; "and Thomas and Charles are giving you their money, eh? and that's all you've got ?"

"Yes, sir. I can't work myself, because I've got the baby and the others to look after."

"Well, my dear," says the chairman, " I am very sorry for you, but your brothers can only have half-time or come back to school."

The girl says nothing, she is only fifteen, and can't argue it out with the gentleman-so she curtseys and is ushered out. I wonder, if the mother dies and the father gets a long term of imprisonment, what the fate of the family will be?

I have said that the hardships entailed upon the poor by the Education Act are numerous. Let me quote a few statistics gleaned from the papers which I turn over on the chairman's desk by his kind permission.

They are cases in which the parents apply to have the fees remitted because they cannot afford to pay them.

1. Mrs. Walker. 7 children of school age, fee 2d. a week each. Total earnings of entire family 10s. Rent 5s. 6d. Husband once good mechanic, host employment through illness and deafness. Parish relief none. Character good. Is now a hawker - sells oranges and fish.

Children half-starved. When an orange is too bad to sell they have it for breakfast, with a piece of bread.

2. Mr. Thompson. 5 children of school age. Out of work. No income but pawning clothes and goods. Rent 4s. Wife drinks surreptitiously. Husband, good character.

3. Mr ——- 5 children of school age; widow. Earnings 6s. Rent 3s. Her husband when alive was a Drury Lane clown. Respectable woman; feels her poverty very keenly.

4. Mr. Garrard. 8 children of school age; two always under doctor. No income. Pawning last rags. Rent 5s. 6d. No parish relief. Starving. Declines to go into workhouse.

I could multiply such instances by hundreds. These, however, will suffice to show how serious a burden is added to the lives of the very poor by the enforced payment of school fees. As a rule they are remitted for very good and sufficient reasons.

How these people live is a mystery. It is a wonder that they are not found dead in their wretched dens, for which they pay a rent out of all proportion to their value, by dozens daily. But they live on, and the starving children come day after day to school with feeble frames and bloodless bodies, and the law expects them to learn as readily as well-fed, healthy children, to attain the same standard of proficiency in a given time.

It is these starving children who are not allowed to earn money towards their support until they are thirteen, and in many cases fourteen. Less necessitous children, as a rule, pass out of school earlier, for reasons which will be obvious to any one who reflects for a moment upon the relationship of a healthy brain to a healthy body.

In another Chapter we shall hear a few more personal narrations at a "B" meeting. I will conclude this one with a picture of a young gentleman whose excuse for non-attendance is at least dramatic. He has been absent for six weeks, and his mother explains, "It's all along of is aven a reglar engagement at the Surrey Pantermine, and there hev been so many matynees."

A BUDDING PRO.

"He's on the Surrey, is he?" says the chairman. "Perhaps that's the reason he can't pass the Standard!"

We see the joke and chuckle, but the boy doesn't.

Evidently his pantomime training has been thrown away upon him.

CHAPTER V.

The ladies and gentlemen whom I had the pleasure of introducing to you in the last chapter, had, most of them, some good and sufficient excuse for the non-attendance of their children at school. Before the "B" meeting at which we assisted was over, more than one case was examined, which left the official no option but to take out a summons and run the risk of one of those amiable lectures which unthinking magistrates now and again see fit to bestow upon the luckless officer of the Board who has done what the law compels him to do, and no more.

The parents summoned are in many instances dissolute or careless people, who utterly neglect their offspring, and take no pains to ensure their attending school, or they are crafty, cunning wretches, who see in the law a means of attaining a consummation devoutly to be wished.

THE TRUANT'S MAMMA.

Here is a woman who, when asked why her boy of nine has not been to school for a month, declares that he plays truant, and that he is quite beyond her control. Now the result of such a complaint is, that the young gentleman will, if the parent reiterates in court her statement, be sent to a reformatory for five years.

That is just what the good lady wants. Her story is one that may be instructive if not edifying.

Two years ago her husband got ten years' penal servitude or a heavy fracture of his country's laws, leaving her with three children, two boys and a girl. There is a custom in such districts as that of which I write which shortens the period of mourning for a lost mate very considerably. Directly husband "No. 1" gets forcibly removed from the domestic hearth, his place is almost invariably taken by another gentleman, who is master of the situation, and *locum tenens* with full family honours.

I cannot resist telling a little story *a propos* of this domestic phase of slum life, which illustrates it rather forcibly. A little girl of eight at one of the schools near the Mint came one morning with a pair of boots on her little feet. This was the first pair of boots she had ever been seen in, and the unwonted magnificence naturally attracted attention.

"Why, Annie, you've got a pair of boots at last, then!" exclaimed the governess.

"Yes, mistress," the child replied," glancing proudly at the battered, second-hand shoes, three times too large for her.

"And where did you get them?"

"One of my fathers gave 'em to me, mistress; the one what's at home this week."

This "father" was evidently a better fellow than most of the nomadic husbands who wander about from family circle to family circle, ready to replace its absent head at a moment's notice. He must have been more generous to another man's child than the "husband" of the lady whose history I have so unceremoniously interrupted, and who wants her boy put away in a reformatory.

Husband "No. 2," I gather from one who knows the history of the case, is a young fellow who objects to "brats," and the "brats" are being got out of the way one by one. The eldest boy was put to thieving, and he is being kept now by the State; the girl took to something worse, and a benevolent society relieved the mother of any future liability on her behalf. And now the good lady comes to the "B" meeting and declares the youngest boy is incorrigible, and hints as broadly as she dare that she should be glad to have him put away as well. She will have her wish, and the boy, whom in all probability she has wilfully kept away and encouraged in his incorrigibleness, will be sent to a reformatory within a fortnight.

Thus you see a wholesale clearance has been made of one family, and the room they took up at home will soon be utilized by new-comers, in the shape of family number two.

A more charming and ingenious way of disposing of incumbrances it is difficult to imagine. It is not, however, by any means uncommon.

Marriage, as an institution, is not fashionable in these districts. Yet so long as cohabitation is possible, that is to say, so long as neither the hospital, the prison, nor the churchyard effects a separation, the couples are fairly faithful, and look upon themselves as man and wife, with the usual marital obligations.

Both parties to the arrangement exhibit great reluctance to "break" of their own free will, and it is marvellous to see the tenacity with which a decent hard-working woman will cling to a ruffian who spends her earnings and blackens her eye, as regularly as Saturday night comes round although he has not the slightest legal claim on her allegiance.

If you ask the couples who live happily together why they don't get married, some will tell you frankly that they never gave it a thought, others that it's a lot of trouble and they haven't had time. A clergyman's wife who took intense interest in a young couple living together in a room in the Mint determined to make them get married. The young fellow earned fair wages, and was sober and steady the girl kept her room and her two little children clean and decent, and was always civil-spoken and pleasant. The good lady who had the *entrée* of the place talked to the young man whenever she saw him, and he admitted at last that, perhaps, the union might as well be made a legal one -"Not that me and Sall 'ull get on any better, you know, mum, - we couldn't ; but since you've been on at her she seems to have a bit o' fancy like for to have the marridge lines, and if you'll tell us how, we'll get it done and over, rnissis."

Delighted with the promise, the lady set to work and prepared everything. She gave the bride a new gown to be married in, and made frocks for the two little ones to come and see their father married; she arranged with her husband to perform the ceremony, and last, but most important, she got the young man a day's holiday without loss of pay from his employers.

The eventful day arrived; the good soul beaming and elated, waited, with a few friends invited to see the interesting ceremony, at the church. The clergyman stood with his book at the altar, but no young couple. Twelve o'clock struck, the clergyman went into the vestry, and put his coat on; and bitterly disappointed at the failure of her little scheme, the good lady sat on for an hour, thinking some delay might have occurred, but after a while she gave it up as a bad job, and departed also.

That evening, in as towering a rage as a clergyman's wife could decently be, she marched off to the Mint, and tackled the delinquents at once. "What did they mean by it?"

The young man was very civil and very apologetic. "He didn't mean to be rude, but the fact was, a mate hearin' he'd got a day off offered him a job at carting as was worth five bob; and you know, mum, I couldn't loose five bob just for the sake o' gettin' married."

I am happy to say that the energetic lady set to work again, got another holiday for the man a week after, and this time "personally conducted " the wedding party to the church, which they did not leave till the young woman was the proud possessor of that by no means common property in the locality, a marriage certificate.

But to return to the "B" meeting. The lady who wants her little boy put away having been disposed of, a decent- looking woman takes her place. She is nursing a baby, and by her side stands a small boy with staring eyes that seem fixed upon nothing in particular - a strange, uncanny, big-headed child, who attracts attention directly.

Mrs. Jones, the mother, is called upon to say why this lad's sister, aged ten, has been absent three weeks.

"Well, I'm very sorry, gen'lemen, but I've had to keep her at house. Ye see, gen'lemen, I haves ruernatics, which takes me all of a nonplush in the joints o' the knees and the ankles of the feet, and then I can't move."

"Yes, but that needn't keep the girl at home. You can nurse the baby even if you have rheumatics."

"Yes, sir, I know ; but it's that boy as is the trouble. Ye see, sir, he can't be lef' not a minnit without somebody as can get after him quick. He's allers scttin' hisself a-fire. He gets the matches wherever we 'ides em, and he lights anything he sees - the bed, the baby, hisself. Bless you, gen'lemen, it's orful ; he can't be off settin' somethin' alight not five minnits together. He ain't right in is ed, sir."

The idiot incendiary paid not the slightest attention ; his wild, strange eyes were wandering about the room, probably for a box of matches with which to set us alight, and make one big blaze of the "B" meeting, chairman, officers, himself, and all.

"And that ain't all, sir: my 'usband's dead, sir; and all we ye got for a livin's a little shop, sir, where we sells drippin', and matches, and candles, and odds and ends; and I can't run in and out when I'm so queer, and the gal's all I've got to do things. I wish you would give her half-time, sir."

A YOUTHFUL INCENDIARY.

The poor woman certainly had her work cut out, with the rheumatics, the baby, the shop, and the idiot incendiary; and the chairman, after a little consultation with the officer, finding the case was a deserving one, granted the half-time; and the woman left evidently considerably relieved, dragging the young gentleman with a tendency to commit hourly arson after her.

The next to put in an appearance was a lady with a wretched-looking face and a shabby, draggled, out-all-night and drunk-in-the-morning appearance generally. Her profession was stated with official bluntness in the paper handed to the chairman. It is generally translated "street-walker" in family circles.

But, whatever she might be, she had children, and the law required them to come to school. Instead of making their attendances, learning to read and write, the children were street Arabs. The woman was meek and quiet enough. She promised "She'd see to it,"

49

and was reminded that she had made the same promise before. This time it was not accepted, and the woman was informed that she would have to appear before a magistrate.

SHE PROMISED "SHE'D SEE TO IT."

Meekly and quietly she said, "Thank you, sir," as if the chairman had presented her with a medal or a pound of tea, and went out.

The women poured in one after the other - there were very few men, most of them, I suppose, being "at work," whatever that term might imply in their particular case - and they were of all sizes, sorts, and conditions. There were respectable; decent, motherly-looking souls, drunken outcasts, slatternly trollops, half-starved and sickly-looking women, and fat, overwhelming women, who came not to be crushed, but to crush.

One gaunt, fierce-looking lady, with the voice of a man and the fist of a prize-fighter, gave the company a bit of her mind. "Her 'gal' warn't a-coming to be worried with a lot o' stuff. She was delikit, her gal was, and the School Board was murderin' of her."

"What's the matter with her?" asked the chairman.

"Well, it's nervis system, and her teeth growin' out."

"Where's the doctor's certificate that she's too ill to attend?"

"Sitifkit? d'ye think I've got time to go a-gettin' sitifkits - not me - ain't my word good ernuff?"

The School Board officer knows this lady's circumstances, and he whispers something to the chairman. The girl's "nervis system" and dental eccentricities have not prevented her affectionate mother from sending her out hawking every day while she stops at home and drinks.

"Where's your husband?" asked the officer. "I haven't seen him lately. He'll have to be summoned, you know, as you can't get a certificate."

The officer in question has good reason to ask affectionately after the husband. Last year the worthy gentleman got a month for playfully tossing the officer down a flight of hairs on to his head.

"Where's my husband ? Ah ! " says she, purple with passion, " you want to summon him, do you ? Well, then, you jolly well carn't. Gord's got him."

"Dead?" asked the chairman. " Yes - didn't I say so?"

"Then you will be summoned instead."

The lady didn't retire - she had to be diplomatically crowded out, and the last sounds that reached the room as she receded along the corridor, under gentle pressure, were wishes that the chairman and all concerned might go where, at least if her estimate of his whereabouts was correct, they would not have the pleasure of meeting her late lamented consort.

There are some rough customers to deal with in this district - so rough that it is a wonder the Act works so smoothly as it does. The fiercest and most reckless of the lawless classes have to be bearded in their dens by the devoted ill-paid officers, who ferret out the children and insist upon their coming to school. Up to the topmost garret and down to the lowest cellar, in dens and hovels given over to thieves and wantons, I have accompanied a School Board officer on his rounds, and I frankly confess that I have passed a few bad quarters of an hour.

"AIN'T MY WORD GOOD ENNUFF?"

There are dozens of these places where the blow follows the word in a moment, where life is held of the least account, and where assaults are so common that the victims would as soon think of asking the police to notice their broken windows as to take cognizance of their broken heads.

There is a legend that one of these cellars in the Mint- it fetches 3s. a week rent, by the by- a man killed a woman and left her; and that nobody took any notice until the body got unpleasant, and then they threw it out into the street. The "'appy dossers " are the wretched people who roam about the street houseless, and creep in to sleep on the stairs, in the passages and untenanted cellars of the lodging-horses with the doors open night and day. No policeman's lantern is ever turned on them, and they crowd together in their rags and make a jolly night of it. Sometimes in among them creeps a starving woman, to die from want and exposure ; and she dies while the foul oath and the ribald jests go on; and the "dossers" who are well enough to be "'appy" make such a noise that a lodger, disturbed in his legitimate rest for which he has paid, comes out and lays about him vigorously at the "varmints," and kicks them down stairs, if he can.

Thus not only are many of the licensed lodging-houses and homes of the poor breeding-houses in themselves for crime, disease, and filth, but they are, for lack of supervision, receptacles for that which has already been bred elsewhere, and which is deposited gratis, to swell the collection.

"'APPY DOSSERS."

A "'appy dosser" can make himself comfortable anywhere. I heard of one who used to crawl into the, dust-bin, and pull the lid down; but I know that to be an untruth, from the simple fact that none of the dust bins on this class of property have a lid. The contents are left, too, for months to decompose, not only under the eyes of the authorities, but under the noses of the inhabitants. The sanitary inspection of these houses is a farce, and in many cases the vestrymen, who ought to put the law in motion, are themselves the owners of the murder-traps.

How foul, how awful some of these places, where the poor have found their last refuge, from Artisans' Dwelling Acts and Metropolitan improvements, are, I dare not tell you. I have been told that the readers of a shilling book don't care to know, and the difficulties of dealing with this subject are increased by my knowledge of the fact that in a truthful account of " How the Poor Live" there can be but little to attract those who read for pleasure only. Rags - that is to say, the rags of our cold, sunless clime - are never picturesque ; squalor and misery can only be made tolerable by the touch of the romancist - and here I dare not romance.

Bad, however, as things are, shocking as is the condition in which thousands and thousands of our fellow-citizens live from the cradle to the grave, it is not an unmixed evil if out of its very repulsiveness grows a remedy for at.

It has got now into a condition in which it cannot be left. For very shame England must do something, nay, for self- preservation, which is the most powerful of all human motives. This mighty mob of famished, diseased, and filthy helots is getting dangerous, physically, morally, politically dangerous. The barriers that have kept it back are rotten and giving way, and it may do the State a mischief if it not looked to in time. Its fevers and its filth may spread to the homes of the wealthy ; its lawless armies may sally forth and give us a taste of the lesson the mob has tried to teach now and again in Paris, when long years of neglect have done their work.

Happily there is a brighter side. Education - compulsory education - has done much. The new generation is learning at least to be clean if not to be honest. The young mothers of the slums - the girls who have been at the Board Schools - have far tidier homes already than their elders. The old people born and bred in filth won't live out of it. If you gave some of the slumites Buckingham Palace they would make it a pigstye in a fortnight. These people are irreclaimable, but they will die out, and the new race can be worked for with hope and with a certainty of success. Hard as are some of the evils of the Education Act, they are outbalanced by the good, and it is that Act above all others which will eventually bring about the new order of things so long desired.

So important a bearing on the home question has the schooling of the children who are to be the rent-payers of the next generation, that I propose to devote the next chapter to sonic sketches of School Board life and character ; and I will take it in one of the worst districts in London, where the parents are sunk in a state of misery almost beyond belief.

I will show you the children at school who come daily to their work from the foulest and dirtiest dens in London - that awful network of hovels which lie about the Borough and the Mint.

CHAPTER VI.

HE difficulty of getting that element of picturesqueness into these Chapters which is so essential to success with a large class of English readers, becomes more and more apparent as I and my travelling companion explore region after region where the poor are hidden away to live as best they can. There is a monotony in the surroundings which became painfully apparent to us, and were our purpose less earnest than it is we might well pause dismayed at the task we have undertaken.

The Mint and the Borough present scenes awful enough in all conscience to be worthy of earnest study; but scene after scene is the same. Rags, dirt, filth, wretchedness, the same figures, the same faces, the same old story of one room unfit for habitation yet inhabited by eight or nine people, the same complaint of a ruinous rent absorbing three-fourths of the toiler's weekly wage, the same shameful neglect by the owner of the property of all sanitary precautions, rotten floors, oozing walls, broken windows, crazy staircases, tile-less roofs, and in and around the dwelling-place of hundreds of honest citizens the nameless abominations which could only be set forth were we contributing to the *Lancet* instead of the *Pictorial World*; -these are the things which confront us, whether we turn to the right or to the left, whether we linger in the Mint or seek fresh fields in the slums that lie round Holborn, or wind our adventurous footsteps towards the network of dens that lie within a stone's-throw of our great National Theatre, Drury Lane.

The story of one slum is the story of another, and all are unrelieved by the smallest patch of that colour which lends a charm to pictures of our poorest peasantry. Cod made the country, they say, and man the town and wretched as is the lot of the agricultural labourer, the handiwork of Heaven still remains to give some relief to the surroundings of his miserable life. Field and tree and flower, the green of the meadow and the hedge, the gold and white of buttercup and daisy, the bright hues of the wild cottage garden,- it is in the midst of these the pigstyes of the rustic poor are pitched, and there is scope for the artist's brush. But in the slums he can use but one colour; all is a monotone - a sombre grey deepening into the blackness of night. Even the blue that in the far-off skies seems to defy the man-made town to be utterly colourless, is obscured by the smoke belched forth from a hundred chimneys ; and when the sun, which shines with systematic impartiality on the righteous and unrighteous alike, is foiled in its efforts to get at these outcasts by the cunning builders, who have put house so close to house that even a sunbeam which had trained down to the proportions of Mddle. Sarah Bernhardt, and then been flattened by a steamroller, could not force its way between the overhanging parapets with any chance of getting to the ground. So what sunshine there is stops on the roofs among the chimney-pots, and is the sole property of the cats of the neighbourhood, who may be seen dozing about in dozens or indulging in a pastime which they have certainly not learnt of their masters and mistresses, namely, washing their faces.

The cat-life of the slums is peculiar. Dogs are rare, but the cats are as common as blackberries in September. Not over clean and not over fat, the cats of the slums yet seem perfectly contented, and rarely leave the district in which they have been reared. They ascend to the roof early in the day, and stay there long after darkness has set in, and in the choice of a local habitation they show their feline sense. The rooms of their respective owners offer, neither air nor sunshine, and when "the family" are all at home, it is possibly the inability of finding even a vacant corner to curl up in that drives Thomas to that part of a house which the people of the East consider the best, but which the people of our East have never sought to utilise.

The cats of the slums are certainly domesticated: they marry and have families, and the kittens are the only really pretty things we have seen since we start on our explorations.

The young of most animals are interesting and picturesque; but a kitten is perhaps the prettiest of all; and a painful contrast is there between the sallow dirty face, the sunken eyes and wizard features of a baby we see sitting on a doorstep nursing one, and the dainty face, blue eyes, and plump pretty figure of the kitten. The mother of the latter has set an example in the matter of philoprogenitiveness and domestic forethought which the mother of the former would do well to imitate.

There are not wanting those who believe that for the present generation of poor little can be done. I mean, of course, the poor who are sunk in the misery and degradation of slum life. Dirtiness is ingrained in them, and if they had decent habitations provided for them to-morrow, they would no more live in them than a gipsy could settle down under any but a canvas roof.

Thrift they do not understand, and are too old to be taught; and ordinary decency is a thing of which they have about as much conception as they would have of the aestheticism of Mr. Oscar Wilde or the philosophy of Mr. Herbert Spencer.

ONE REMOVE FROM AN HOUSE.

I am not of the school which says that the regeneration of the masses is hopeless, but I freely confess that the great chance of bringing about a new and better order of things lies among the children who are to be the mothers and fathers of the future. In the old Biblical times water and fire were the elements which solved the knotty problem of regenerating a seething mass of humanity sunk in the lowest abysses of vice and degradation. The deluge that shall do the work now must come of the opening of the floodgates of knowledge. Already, in tiny rivulets as yet, the waters are trickling even into the darkest corners of our great cities. The flood can never rise high enough to cleanse those who have grown up ignorant, - at best it can but wet their feet; but the children cannot escape it,- the waters will gather force and volume and grow into a broad glorious river, through which the boys and girls of to-day will wade breast high until they gain the banks of the Promised Land.

PRETTY INTELLIGENT.

It is this river of knowledge which the modern wanderers in the wilderness must ford to reach the Canaan which the philanthropist sees waiting for them in his dreams.

The first working of the Education Act was fraught with countless difficulties. It was no light task to catch the children of a shifting race, to schedule street Arabs and the offspring of beggars and thieves and prostitutes. But in the course of a few years almost every difficulty has been conquered, and now there is hardly a child above a certain age - no matter how wretched its condition may be - that is not brought within the beneficial influence of education.

True that many of them come shoeless, ragged, and starving, to learn the three R's, to burthen their scanty brains with sums and tasks while their stomachs are empty and their bodies weakened by disease and neglect; but they have at least their chance. Let us take a school where, perhaps, the poorest children come-a school recruited from such homes as we have familiarised you, with in previous chapters - and see the little scholars at their dainty tasks. Here is a child who is but one remove from an idiot. The teacher has a hard task, for the Government inspector expects all the scholars to make the same progress. This poor waif - the offspring of a gentleman whose present address is Holloway Gaol, and a lady who has been charged seventy-three times with being drunk and incapable - must pass a certain standard before she can leave school; in her case, if she lives, she will pass out by age, for statistics show that no system can make this class of intellect retain a lesson. It is sowing seed upon a rock, and there will be no harvest; but the child has just sufficient intelligence to escape the asylum, and between the asylum and the school there is no half-way house.

Some benefit, at least, she derives from the discipline, the care, and the motherly sympathy of a kind head-mistress, who takes a strong personal interest in her little charges. For so many hours a day at least the child escapes the ghastly surroundings of the den which is her "home."

Side by side with her sits a pretty, intelligent little girl of nine. This child's eyes are bright with intelligence, the features are pleasing and regular. As she is called forward, she rises and smilingly comes towards us. There is none of that stolid indifference, that mechanical obedience to a command which distinguishes too many of the little ones who are here in obedience to the laws. This girl learns quickly, and has had all the better qualities brought out. She is neat, and takes a pride in her personal appearance. She has learnt to be ashamed of dirt, and she is ambitious to be high up in her class. Ambition is the one quality which will help above all others to lift the poor out of degradation. The older race have it not ; hence they are content with their present positions, only seeking to gratify their daily appetites, and caring not a fig for the morrow. This child will do well, whatever she undertakes ; and it is such as she who will survive in the battle of life, and become the mothers of a better and more useful class.

Yet hers is a sad enough story. Her father was a boatman, and in a drunken rage struck his wife down with a boat hook.

Hers was the common offence of asking for money. The blow injured the woman's brain, and from that day to this she has been in a lunatic asylum. The father disappeared after the crime, and the child's grandmother took the orphan with living parents in, and out of her scanty earnings kept her. One day this year the old lady passed some men carrying a body found in the river to the dead-house. Curiosity induced her to go in with the crowd, and the face of the dead man was that of her son.

A back street tragedy-common enough, with a varied plot and incidents in these parts, but, as it stands, the life-story of this child.

"And your granny keeps you now? " says the teacher, as she concludes the little history and turns to the girl.

"Yes, teacher; and when I grow up I'm going to keep granny."

So may it be!

Here is a group of girls sketched hastily from the hundred in the room. Some of them come from decent homes, and sonic from cellars ; many of their histories arc romances, but they are romances which mostly tend one way-to show the misery, the guilt, and the poverty in which they have been reared ; and to recount them would be but to dwell upon a note which perhaps I have touched too often already.

There are brighter stories, too, to he told of their parents, but none so bright as they will be able to tell of themselves when, after years of discipline and culture, they go forth to lead lives which with their fathers and mothers were impossible.

Close to the school where the either girls are educated, and in the same building, is the department for infants. Here the children under seven are prepared to pass into the upper department.

Directly we enter we are struck with the appearance of these children. Bad faces there are among them - bruises and scars, and bandages and rags - but the bulk of these younger children have a generally *better* appearance than their little neighbours.

There is a theory in the school, and it is borne out to a certain extent by fact, that some of the youngest and best-looking are the children of girls who just got the benefit of the Education Act before they were too old, and who in their young married life have reaped the benefit of those principles of cleanliness and thrift which the Board School inculcates. The young mothers are already a race far ahead of the older ones in this district, and the children naturally benefit by it. It must be borne in mind that the girls of this class marry or take a mate at a very early age. Many of them have three or four children by the time they are twenty, so that at the time the Education Act came into force, some twelve years ago, they would have been brought under its influence. These young women, too, live in a better way; their room is tidier and cleaner, there is a little coquetry in them, and they have a sense of shame which renders them excellent service. They are anxious about their children's education, they recognise the advantage the discipline and instruction have been to them, and the general tone of their lives is every way a distinct advance on the old order of things.

I quote these facts because they so fully bear out the theory that Education must be the prime instrument in changing the condition of the poor for the better, whatever results it may have later on upon the condition of the labour market and the political and social questions of the future. The many theories which are put forward about the result of educating the masses, it is not nay province here to discuss; nor need I consider those doctrines which are closely akin to socialism, and which are the favourite arguments of a school of advanced thinkers when discussing the future condition of the masses.

I have only to confine myself to the facts before me, and I think this great improvement in the children of the young mothers a most important one.

The best examples are in a room which is a kind of *creche*. Here the babies can be left by the mothers who have to go out to work, and the tiny mites are looked after with motherly care by a kind-hearted creature whose lot I do not envy. Fancy forty infants, some of them little over two years old, to take care of for eight hours a day. Mothers will appreciate the situation better than I can describe it.

Look at the illustration on the next page, and you will see the babies at dinner. They have brought their bread and butter with them, and they sit at the little low table enjoying it thoroughly. In the winter, when work is scarce, alas! baby's bread and butter is not always so thick as it is to-day. Sometimes baby has only a dry crust. But there is a lot of the best sort of Christian character knocking about in the Great City, and an excellent society, which provides dinners for poor Board School children, has done much to alleviate this painful state of things. A starving body, a famished child there is no fear of imposture here; and if any one who reads these Chapters wishes to support a truly admirable movement, where there is no fear of abuse, he or she may imitate Captain Cuttle, and, having found a good thing, make a note of it.

In addition to the dining and play-table there is a long bed in the room. There the tired babies sleep eight or ten in a row sometimes, and forget their baby troubles. The *creche* as a boon and a blessing to the poor woman who going out to work has a choice of keeping an elder girl at home to nurse the baby and be summoned for it, or locking the said baby up alone in a room all day with the risk to its life and its himb~ inevitable to such a course, not to mention the danger of fire and matches and fits.

It is therefore with grief I hear that there are to be no more built in Board Schools, and that the cost of maintaining those existing must in future be defrayed by voluntary contributions. The Government objects to the *creche* department on economical grounds.

The lady who manages the infants old enough to learn has no easy task, but the order is perfect, and the children drill like little soldiers. Here, too, the stories of many of them reveal a depth of misery not often sounded except in the police-courts.

FIVE.

Here is a bright, pretty, golden-haired girl of five who rather upsets my pet theory. She ought to be ugly and dull, if there is anything in breed. Her mamma is seldom out of prison for more than a week. Mamma not having learned Latin does not know the difference between *meum* and *tuum,* and is an incorrigible shoplifter and thief. When she is enjoying her liberty, too, she has a habit of tumbling about which is not conducive to health. She has fallen out of a window and damaged the pavement below, and once with a baby in her arms she fell down the stairs of this very school.

When they picked her up the baby's collar bone was broken, but she was sound enough to exclaim, "If it hadn't ha' been for that blessed baby i'd a broken my neck, I would."

It isn't every mother who is philosopher enough to recognise the use of a baby in breaking her fall down stairs.

The father of this little girl, whose counterfeit presentment is here given, is a respectable man; but he has to go a long way away for work, and when papa is in the country and mamma is in goal, some good Sisters of Charity have taken the child and found it a home.

We have made our notes and taken our sketches, and the children file out of school to dinner and to play.

One sturdy little chap takes his sister's hand and leads her out like a little father. He has over half a mile to take her home. We are told it is a beautiful sight to see him piloting her across the great thoroughfares when the traffic sweeps wildly up and down, and never leaving go the little hand that is placed so trustingly in his till home is reached and the dangers of the streets are over. They are a pretty pair as they toddle out hand in hand, and they form a pleasant picture in this brief sketch of the little scholars who come daily from the garrets and cellars of the slums to get that "little learning which in their cases is surely the reverse of a "dangerous thing."

A PRETTY PAIR.

CHAPTER VII.

If I were asked to say off-hand what was the greatest curse of the poor and what was the greatest blessing, I think my answer to the first query would be the public-house, and to the second the hospital. Of course, I might be wrong. There are some people who will contend that in these islands the greatest blessing of the natives of all degrees is that they are Great Britons. Our patriotic songs bid us all rejoice greatly at the fact, and patriotism is not a class privilege. The starved outcast, crouching for shelter on a wild March night in one of the stone recesses of London Bridge, has a right to exclaim with the same pride as the Marquis of Westminster-

"Far as the breeze can bear the billows' foam,

Survey our empire and behold our home."

His soul, for all we know, may rejoice greatly that Britannia rules the waves, and in spite of the fact that a policeman spying him out as "without the visible means of subsistence" may seize him and consign him to durance vile, he - the outcast, not the policeman - may ponder with much national vanity on the fact that Britons never shall be slaves.

Out upon the parochial-minded disciples of the Birmingham school, who pretend that a nation can be very great abroad and yet very small at home! "Survey our Empire" is a noble line, and there is another about the Queen's morning drum which has a magnificent ring about it, and crops up in patriotic leading articles about twice a week all the year round. It is, however, just possible that the vast extent of British rule does not come home so pleasurably to my friend on the bridge as it does to the well-fed, prosperous citizen of Jingo proclivities who believes that Heaven's first command to an Englishman was, "Thou shalt remove thy neighbour's landmark." The poor wretch may "survey" his "empire" with a feeling of anything but contentment, and he may be tempted to wish that we had a little less empire to look after abroad in order that a little attention might be bestowed upon the place where charity begins.

Even at the risk of being pronounced unpatriotic, I shall, therefore, maintain my contention that the greatest blessing of the poor is the hospital - that noble institution of which Englishmen of all classes and all creeds may reasonably be proud.

Sickness, disease, and accident enter very largely into the annals of the poor. Overcrowding, and unsanitary dwellings - all the ghastly surroundings of poor life in a great city, which I have attempted feebly to describe in these papers - render the masses peculiarly susceptible to illness in every shape and form. Epidemics of some sort or other are rarely absent from the poorer districts, and many painful diseases and deformities are transmitted regularly from parent to child. To be sound of limb and well in health in these dens is bad enough, but the existence of an invalid under such circumstances is pitiable to a degree. The hospitals are the heavens-upon-earth of the poor. I have heard little children - their poor pinched faces wrinkled with pain - murmur that they didn't mind it, because if they had been well they would never have come to "the beautiful place." Beautiful, indeed, by contrast with their wretched homes are the clean wards, the comfortable beds, and the kind faces of the nurses. Step across from the home of a sick child in the slums of the Borough to the Evelina Hospital, and it is like passing from the infernal regions to Paradise. To this noble charity little sufferers are often brought dirty, neglected, starving; and even the nurses, used as they are to such sights, will tell you their hearts ache at the depth of baby wretchedness revealed in some of the cases brought to them. Passing from cot to cot, and hearing the histories of the little ones lying there so clean, and, in spite of their suffering, so happy, one is inclined to think that the charity is a mistake - that to nurse these children back to health only to send them again to their wretched homes us a species of refined cruelty. It were better in dozens of cases that the children were left to die now, while they are young and innocent, than that death should be wrestled with and its prize torn from it only to be cast back into a state of existence which is worse than death. The children have some dim inkling of this themselves. Many of them cry when they are well, and cling to the kind nurses, asking piteously not to be sent back to the squalor and dirt, and often, alas ! cruelty, from which they have been snatched for a brief spell. Here is a child at home and the same child in the hospital. Contrast the surroundings. Look on this picture and on that, and then say if there is not at least some ground for such a train of thought as the Hospital for Sick Children suggested to me!

The elder people doubtless appreciate the blessings of the hospital as much as the children. The poor generally speak in the highest terms of such institutions. They could not, as a rule, lie ill at home ; care and attention would be impossible; and for a sick person the atmosphere would mean certain death. Doctors they cannot afford to pay. The class of practitioners who lay themselves out for business in these neighbourhoods are not, as a rule, much more than nostrum and patent-medicine vendors, and their charges are generally extortionate. If you could bring yourself to imagine truthfully the condition of the sick poor without the hospitals to go to, you would see a picture of human misery so appalling that you would cover your eyes and turn away from it with a shudder. Yet there are such pictures to be seen. There are cases which, from varying circumstances, do not go to the hospital. There are men and women who lie and die day by day in these wretched single rooms, sharing all the family trouble, enduring the hunger and the cold, and waiting without hope, without a single ray of comfort, until God curtains their staring eyes with the merciful film of death.

It was such a case we came upon once in our wanderings, and which, without unduly harrowing the reader up, I will endeavour to describe.

The room was no better and no worse than hundreds of its class. It was dirty and dilapidated, with the usual bulging blackened ceiling, and the usual crumbling greasy walls. Its furniture was a dilapidated four-post bedstead, a chair, and a deal table. On the bed lay a woman, young and with features that before hourly anguish contorted them had been comely. The woman was dying slowly of heart disease. Death was "writ large" upon her face. At her breast she held her child, a poor little mite of a baby that was drawing the last drain of life from its mother's breast. The day was a bitterly cold one; through the broken casement the wind came ever and anon in icy gusts, blowing the hanging end of the ragged coverlet upon the bed to and fro like a flag in a breeze. The wind roared in the chimney too, eddying down into the fireless grate with a low howling noise like the moan of a Banshee round a haunted house. To protect the poor woman from the cold her husband had flung on it his tattered great coat - a garment that the most ancient four-wheel night cabman would have spurned as a knee protector. " He was a plumber," she whispered to us in a weak, hollow voice; "he had been out of work for a week, and he had gone out to try and look for a job." One shivered to think of him wearily trudging the streets this bitter day, half clad and wholly starved; what must have been his torture as he failed at place after place, and the day wore on and brought the night when he would have to return to the poor dying wife with the old sad story?

As one realised the full meaning of this little domestic tragedy, and knew that it was only one of many daily enacted in the richest city in the world - the scene of it laid not a mile from the full tide of all the pomps and vanities of fashion, of all the notorious luxury and extravagances which is the outward show of our magnificence and wealth, it was hard to repress a feeling of something akin to shame and anger - shame for the callous indifference which bids one half the world ignore the sufferings of the other-anger that with all the gold annually borne along on the broad stream of charity so little of it ever reaches the really deserving and necessitous poor.

The house this poor woman lay dying in was one of a block which would have been a prize to a sanitary inspector anxious to make a sensational report. For the room in question the plumber out of work had to pay four and six-pence, and the broken pane of glass the landlord had refused to replace. The man was told "he must do it himself, or if he didn't like it as it was he could go."

Such stories as this are painful, but they should be told. It is good for the rich that now and again they should he brought face to face with misery, or they might doubt its existence. These people - our fellow-citizens - cannot be neglected with impunity. These fever and pestilence- breeding dens that are still allowed to exist, these death-traps out of which vestrymen and capitalists make large annual incomes, are a danger to the whole community.

While I am on this subject, I may as well quote an instance which bears directly upon the interest - the selfish interest - which the better classes have in lending their voices to swell the chorus of complaints which is going up about the present state of things.

Here is an "interior" to which I would call the special attention of ladies who employ nurse-girls for their children. This room when we entered it was in a condition beyond description. The lady was washing the baby, and she made that an excuse for the dirt of everything else. Two ragged boys were sitting on the filthy floor, a dirty little girl was in a corner pulling a dirty kitten's tail, and the smoke from the untidiest grate I ever saw in my life was making the half-washed baby sneeze its little head nearly off. The family, all told, that slept in this room was seven. There was a bed and there was a sofa - so I concluded the floor must have been the resting-place of some of them. "The eldest girl" - materfamilias informed us in answer to our questions - was gone out. She slept on the sofa. We knew somebody had slept there, because some rags were on it which had evidently done duty as bed-clothes.

Outside this room, which opened on to a back yard, was a dust-bin. We didn't want eyesight to know that - it appealed with sufficient power to another sense. Inside was an odour which made the dust-bin rather a relief.

I have described this place a little graphically for the sake of that eldest girl. It is not from any gallantry to the fair sex that I have done this, but because the young woman in question was, I ascertained, a domestic servant. She was a nursemaid just home from a place at Norwood, and in a week she w'as going to a place at Clapham. I remembered, as I gazed on the scene, a certain vigorous letter from Mr. Charles Reade which appeared in the *Daily Telegraph* some years ago about servants "pigging with their relations at home," and wanting the best bed-room and a feather-bed with damask furniture when in service. I never so thoroughly realised what "pigging with their relations" meant before.

Now if you will take the trouble to think out the possible result of girls going from such pigstyes as these straight into well-to-do families, where they will nurse the children and be constantly in the closest contact with the younger members of the family, I think you will see that the dangers of unhealthy homes for the poor may be equally dangerous to a better class. I should like to know how many families now mourning the loss of a little child from fever, or the death of some dear one from small-pox, would have been spared their sorrow had the existence of such places as I have described been rendered impossible by the action of the law!

I do not imagine for one moment that I have seen, or that I am likely to see, the worst phases of the evil which has become one of the burning questions of the hour. But what I have written about I have in every case seen with my own eyes, and in no case have I exaggerated; and yet more than one of my kindly correspondents doubt my story of the dead body being kept and eventually put out into the street.

With regard to this, let the reader in doubt ask any sanitary inspector or officer of health to whom he can get an introduction if it is not an appalling fact that the poor have grown so used to discomfort and horrors that they do not look upon a corpse in the room they live, and eat, and sleep In as anything very objectionable!

It often happens there is no money to pay for the funeral, and so, with that inertness and helplessness bred of long years of neglect, nothing at all is done, no steps are taken, and the body stops exactly where it was when the breath left it.

The following incident I take haphazard from the reports of Dr. Liddle, whose recent statement has even attracted Parliamentary attention and led to a question in the House:-

PROLONGED RETENTION OF A DEAD BODY IN A ROOM OCCUPIED BY A FAMILY.

Mr. Wrack reports that, on visiting No. 17, Hope Street, Spital fields, he found in the room of the second floor the dead body of a child who had died fifteen days before the time of his visit. The room, which contained 1,176 cubic feet of space, was occupied by the parents of the dead child and a daughter aged thirteen years. the body was in a decomposed state. The reason assigned for not burying the child at an earlier period was that the father had no means to do so, and that his friends had failed to render him the assistance which they had promised. Mr. Wrack having pointed out the danger of keeping a dead body so long in the only room occupied by the family, application was made to the relieving officer, and the body was buried on the following day.

Fifteen days! Fancy that! with the knowledge you have by this time of the size and condition of the room in which the corpse remains mixed up with the living inmates day and night. Here are two more cases. Note the fact that in the first the child has died of scarlet fever, and that tailoring work is going on around it-work which when finished will be carried, in all human probability, with the germs of disease in it to the homes of well-to-do and prosperous people - a class which too frequently objects to be worried with revelations of the miseries of the masses.

PROLONGED RETENTION OF A DEAD BODY IN A ROOM OCCUPIED BY A FAMILY.

Mr. Wrack reports that, upon visiting No. 28, Church Street, Spitalfleds, on the 5th December last, he found in the second floor front room the dead body of a child which had died of scarlet fever on the 1st of the month. The body was not coffined, and it lay exposed on a table in one corner of the room. the room was occupied as a living and sleeping room by five persons, viz., the father and mother, their child, a girl about three years old, and by two adults, viz., the grandfather and grandmother of the child, who were engaged at tailors' work. The child was playing on the floor. The room was about fourteen feet square and eight feet high, thus affording only 260 cubic feet of space to each person. The smell on entering the room was most sickening. Upon remonstrating with the people for keeping the body so long unburied, and especially for not having it coffined, they replied that they were waiting to raise the means for burying it and, being Irish, said that it was not heir custom to coffin their dead until the day of the funeral. The body was not buried until the 9th of December, and then it had to be buried by the parish authorities.

Mr. Wrack also visited No. 24, Princes Street, Spitalfields, on the 5th January, and found in the second floor front room the dead body of an aged woman, who died on Christmas Day. The room was occupied by the daughter of the deceased, a person about 40 years of age, who lived and slept in the same room. Upon asking the reason of her keeping the body so long unburied, she stated that she had been waiting for suitable things to be made for the funeral and upon asking when the funeral would take place, she stated that the body would hot be buried until the 8th January, a period of fifteen days from the death. The Board had no power to compel the removal of the corpse, as there is no mortuary belonging to the Board in the district.

I want to drive this nail home, though it is the practice itself I should prefer to knock on the head. Here are three more cases. Let rue quote them, and have done with the subject.

PROLONGED RETENTION OF DEAD BODIES.

There have been three cases of prolonged retention of the dead in rooms occupied as living and sleeping rooms. One of these cases was that of a child who died at No. 26, King Street, Spitalflelds, and whose body was retained for nine days, the parents stating that they were inside to raise sufficient money to bury it. During the time the body was kept it became so offensive that it was necessary to remove it to a shed at the rear of the house. Eventually the father applied to the relieving officer, and obtained an order for the burial of the body. Another case was that of a young man who died of consumption at to, Royal Mint Street. The body of this young man was kept for eight days in the room in which his father and mother lived and slept.

The third case was that of a child three weeks old, who died at No. 5, Devonshire Place, Whitechapel. The body of this child was kept in the room occupied by its parents for a period of twelve days, and at the time of the visit of the inspector the smell from it was most offensive.

Although in each of these cases everything was done by the officer of this Board and by the relieving officer to induce the respective parties to bury their dead before a nuisance was occasioned, yet to a certain extent their efforts were unavailing.

As such cases are of frequent occurrence, it is certainly full time that power was given to magistrates to order the burial without delay of every corpse which is certified to be a nuisance or dangerous to the public health.

It is necessary a great many things were done. It is necessary, above all, that the direct attention of the State should be given to the whole question, but the Home Secretary says there is "no time" to attend to such matters. The question which led to this answer and the Home Secretary's statement in full were as follows:-

SANITARY CONDITION OF WHITECHAPEL.

Mr. Bryce asked the Secretary of State for the Home Department whether his attention had been called to the two last reports presented to the Whitechapel District Board of Works by the Medical Officer of health on the sanitary condition of the Whitechapel district, in which he condemned, as unsanitary and ill-arranged, several new buildings recently erected in that district, and expressed the opinion that amendments in the existing Building Acts were urgently required ; and whether, if sufficient powers to prevent the erection or order the closing of unsanitary dwellings were not now possessed by local authorities, he would undtertake to bring in a Bill to amend the Building Acts in this important particular, by investing the proper local authorities with such powers.

Sir W. Harcourt said he would be glad to introduce Bills upon this sod many other subjects, but there was no time for them. -*Evening Standard,* June 18, 1883.

"No time!"

It is well, with that answer ringing in our ears, to turn to the Parliamentary proceedings and discover what the important questions are which are engrossing the entire attention of the Legislature, and leaving "no time" for such a matter as the constant menace to public health which exists in the present system of "Housing the Poor." I will not enumerate them, or I might be tempted into a political disquisition which would be out of place ; but the reader can, with considerable profit to himself, find them and make a note of them.

The list of important measures which have consumed the session and left "no time" for this question will be instructive and amusing - amusing because the discussions which have taken up the time of the House contain in themselves all the elements of screaming farce.

And talking of screaming farce I am reminded by my collaborator that Mr. J. L. Toole is in his sketch-book, and I have never given an opportunity for him to be introduced yet.

A FAMILIAR FACE.

Room by all means, and at once for Mr. J. L. Toole - not the Toole of Toole's Theatre-the popular comedian who has made tomfoolery a fine art and burlesque a science, but his living, breathing image as he appeared to us, voice, and gesture, at the door of a house at which we lately knocked in search of information as to the profits of hat-box making.

Our J. L Toole didn't tell us - he was very funny - he cracked wheezes that even John Laurence himself might give off without blushing.

He suggested that while we were about it perhaps "he might as well tell us who he worked for as how much he got, and then we could go round and offer to make hat-boxes a halfpenny a dozen under." We didn't get much out of our J. L Toole except his portrait, and that was taken entirely without his permission, and is herewith presented gratis to our readers.

CHAPTER VIII.

ONE of the greatest evils of the overcrowded districts of London is the water supply. I might almost on this head imitate the gentleman who wrote a chapter on Snakes in Iceland, which I quote in its entirety- "There are no snakes in Iceland." To say, however, that in these districts there is no water supply would be incorrect, but it is utterly inadequate to the necessities of the people. In many houses more water comes through the roof than through a pipe, and a tub or butt in the back yard about half full of a black, foul-smelling liquid, supplies some dozens of families with the water they drink and the water they wash in as well. It is, perhaps, owing to the limited nature of the luxury that the use of water both internally and externally is rather out of favour with the inhabitants. As to water for sanitary purposes, there is absolutely no provision for it in hundreds of the most densely-inhabited houses. In the matter of water and air, the most degraded savage British philanthropy has yet adopted as a pet is a thousand times better off than the London labourer and his family, dwelling in the areas whose horrors medical officers are at last divulging to the public.

THE WATER BUTT.

The difficulties of attaining that cleanliness which we are told is next to godliness may be imagined from the contemplation of this butt, sketched in the back yard of a house containing over ninety people.

The little boy in his shirt-sleeves has come to fill his tin bowl, and we are indebted to him for the information that he wants it for his mother to drink. The mother is ill - has been for weeks - her lips are burning with fever, her throat is dry and parched, and this common reservoir, open to all the dust and dirt with which the air is thick, open to the draining in rainy weather of the filthy roof of the tumble-down structure beside it, this is the spring at which she is to slake her thirst. Is it any wonder that disease is rampant, or that the Temperance folk have such trouble to persuade the masses that cold water is a good and healthy drink?

Remember, this is absolutely the supply for the day; it is, perhaps, turned on for about five minutes, and from this butt the entire inhabitants of the house must get all the water they want. In dozens of instances there is n supply at all-accident or design has interfered with it and the housewife who wants to wash her child's face or her own, or do a bit of scrubbing, has to beg of a neighbour or make a predatory excursion into a backyard more blessed than her own.

Some of the facts about the water supply are not easy to deal with in articles for general reading, nor do they lend themselves to the art of the illustrator. The hewer of wood has found plenty of scope in this series, but the difficulties of the "drawer of water" are great. It was while I and my esteemed collaborator were debating how we could possibly reproduce much that we had seen in connection with this crying evil that a gentleman came along and gave us the chance of at least one sketch "on the spot." You observe him busy at the side of a tub - a tub from which his neighbours will fill their drinking and their culinary vessels anon. Do not imagine that he is engaged in his morning ablution. He is washing his potatoes - that is all - and in the evening he will take them out baked, and sell them in the public highway. For the sake of the public I am glad they will be baked, but though the water will in some instances be boiled, I don't think that tea is improved by the dirt off potato-skins - at least I have never heard so.

Perhaps at the house where this tub was sketched the inhabitants were not so much injured as they might have been by the deficient water supply in the yard. If they didn't get water in one way, they generally had it in another. The law of compensation is always at work, and the rapacity of a landlord who left his tenants so badly off in one particular way may have been a godsend in another.

The water in rainy weather simply poured through the roof of this house, saturating the sleepers in their beds and washing their faces in a rough-and-ready manner, but unfortunately it didn't rain towels at the same time, so that the bath had its inconveniences.

The cause of these periodical shower-baths was pointed out to us by a tenant who paid four and sixpence a week for his "watery nest" in the attic, and who, in language which did not tend to show that his enforced cleanlincss had brought godliness in its train, explained that the land lord had taken the lead from the roof and sold it, and replaced it with asphalte, which had cracked with the result above described.

Unacquainted with the stern necessities of the situation, you will contemplate the picture and say that these people are idiots to pay rent for such accommodation. What are they to do? - Move. Whither ? They know well how they will have to tramp from slum to slum, losing work, and the difficulties which will beset them on this room-hunt. They are thankful to have a roof even with cracks in it, and they will go on suffering-not in silence, perhaps, but without taking action, because they know if they go further they may fare worse.

WASHING HIS POTATOES.

The accommodation which these people will put up with is almost incredible.

Some of the houses are as absolutely dangerous to life and limb as those specially built up on the stage as pitfalls for the unwary feet of the melodramatic heroes and heroines led there by designing villains in order that they may fall through traps into dark rivers and so be got rid of.

Here is a house which has been slowly decaying for years; the people who live in it must be competent to accept engagements as acrobats, yet from floor to roof every room is densely inhabited.

The stairs are rotten, and here and there show where some foot has trodden too heavily. The landing above is a yawning gulf which you have to leap, and leap lightly, or the rotten boarding would break away beneath you. Open a door and look into a room. There are two women and three children at work, and the holes in the floor are patched across with bits of old boxes which the tenants have nailed down themselves.

The place is absolutely a shell. There is not a sound a room or passage in it. Yet it is always crammed with tenants, and they pay their rent without a murmur - nay, within the last year the rents of the rooms have been raised a nearly twenty-five per cent.

The gentleman who inhabits the ground-floor with his wife and family is best off. He is a bit of a humorist, and he seems quite proud of pointing out to us the dilapidations of his dwelling-place, and takes the opportunity to indulge in what the gentlemen of the theatrical persuasion call "wheezes."

"Come thro'," he says; " well, no, I can't say as anybody have come through, not altogether. We sees a leg o' somebody sometimes as we ain't invited to join us, and now and agen a lump o' ceilin' comes down when the young woman up stairs stamps her foot, but so long as they don't start a dancin' acadermy up there, I don't mind."

"But haven't you spoken to the landlord about it?"

"Spoke! Lor' bless you! wot's the use? He'd larf at us, and if he was to larf too loud it might be dangerous. He won't do nothink. The place is bound to come down, yer know, by and by, for improvements."

Possibly the man's explanation of the landlord's neglect was correct, but to us it certainly appeared that the place was more likely to come down for lack of improvements. Going to bed under such circumstances as these must require a good deal of confidence, but I suppose the contingency of the floor above descending on one in one's sleep does not have the same terror for these people that it had for the nervous hero of that story of Edgar Allan Poe's, in which the room with contracting walls and descending roof was supposed to be a horror worthy of the inventive genius of the gentlemen of the Inquisition.

Of course, when the ordinary repairs demanded by consideration for the safety of life and limb are left undone, and the most ordinary sanitary precautions are neglected, it is not likely that the present race of poor tenement-owners will listen to the appeals of those tenants whose livelihood - depends upon them keeping animals, and make some provision for the housing of pigs and the stabling of donkeys.

Strange, too, as it may seem, in the houses which are being built on improved principles, no provision is made for the harrows and donkeys of the costermonger - a class which enters very largely into the composition of the one-roomed tribes. Some time ago a man was charged with assaulting his wife, and at the magisterial hearing it was elicited that the matrimonial quarrel was all on account of a donkey which slept under the bed.

The magistrate was naturally astonished. He didn't believe such a state of things possible. Doubtless his wonder was shared by the public. The presence of a donkey in the apartment of a costermonger and his family is, however, by no means rare, and quite recently a zealous sanitary inspector has discovered a cellar inhabited by a man, his wife, three children, *and four pigs.*

The presence of animals not exactly regarded as domestic is a feature of certain poor districts of London. Fowls roost nightly in dozens of bedrooms in the back streets; - and only the other day a score of those miserable tortoises that one sees on barrows destitute of the smallest vestige of green stuff, and probably enduring the most prolonged agony, were discovered crawling about the floor of a costermonger's attic among his progeny, only slightly inferior in point of numbers to the poor animals themselves.

It is a great complaint of the men, who as a rule are hardworking, honest fellows enough in their way, and thrifty too when they can keep away from the temptation of drink, that so little attention is being paid to their needs in the many schemes for improved dwellings for the industrial classes.

In some of the cases where the accommodation for ponies and donkeys may fairly be called "stabling," the entrance is through the passage of a house densely inhabited, and the animals are led in and out daily in such a manner as to be a nuisance to the occupants, while the stables, being so close to the windows of the room and kept in anything but good order, are a constant danger to health.

I have been assured by an old inhabitant of the costers' quarters that he knew a donkey who went upstairs to the third floor every night to go to bed ; but old inhabitants are not to be relied upon, and I give you this story for what it is worth.

Of one thing, however, no one who personally investigates the poorer districts of great cities can remain in doubt. There are there hidden away from general observation marvels as great as any of those which the enterprising Farini imports from the Cannibal islands, the dismal swamps, the deserts and jungles of the savage world, for the amusement and edification of the shilling-paying public. Missing links abound, and monstrosities are plentiful. Some of the terrible sights which we have seen we have too much respect for the readers' feelings to reproduce. Now and again the revelations of some police court send a shudder through society. Children starved and stunted and ignorant as the lowest beasts of the forest are unearthed in foul dens where they have passed their little lives chained to the walls, or pounced upon by the police, led to the discovery by the tavern gossip of the neighbours. Grown women who have lived naked in underground cellars, and long ago lost their reason, are found one fine morning by the merest accident while their gaolers are away. On these hidden horrors of unknown London I need not dwell here. The history of Horrible London has yet to be written, but the brutality which makes many of these terrible things possible is largely due to the circumstances under which the poor live. rue careless disregard of human life and human suffering which has so long characterised us as a nation must bear fruit. The waste of human life brought about by the conditions under which the poor are allowed to live breeds in them a contempt for the sufferings of others. They become hardened, and the cruelty at which we shudder is their second nature. All that is best and holiest in life there is nothing to encourage - only the ferocious instincts of the brute are fostered by a state of existence in which the struggle for the very air men breathe is bitter and intense.

Says a philanthropist, who has gone to the root of this appalling subject:- " In these districts men live in little more than half the space their corpses occupy when dead Think of it. Penetrate the awful places where vice and squalor, crime and brutality reign supreme; where the oath of the gin-maddened ruffian, the cry of the trampled wife, and the wail of the terrified child ring out night and day; where all is one fierce ferment in a hell upon earth, where day brings no light, and night no rest, and ask yourself what manner of fruit these forcing-houses can bear.

When some one bold enough shall write "Horrible London," and the black page lies open that all may read, - then, and not till then, will the enormity of the responsibility be recognised of those to whom the power to do so much has been given and who have done so little.

IN PETTICOATS.

That work is for stronger hands than mine to do. I am content here to chronicle such lights and shadows of life among the poor as fall across my paths in a journey round the outskirts only of the dark continent in our midst. Here is an incident which, pathetic enough, has yet its humorous side. Here is a boy of eight years old in petticoats, a big, strong, healthy lad. His father is a dock labourer, and this is how he was brought forward as a candidate for some cast-off clothing which a director of the East and West India Dock Company was generously distributing.

The dock labourers are a distinct class among the East-end poor, and I hope at some future time to give the reader a glimpse of life among them. How hard their struggle is my be gathered when their boys have to go till eight and mine years old in petticoats because the parents cannot afford to buy them knickerbockers or trousers.

CHAPTER IX.

THESE pages would be incomplete without at least a passing reference to some of the many efforts which have already been made to deal with the evils arising from the condition of things it has been my desire to expose.

The mere charitable work going on I have not space to deal with. There are night refuges, missions, and many excellent institutions due to public and private enterprise in all the poorer quarters, all of which in a manner more or less satisfactory afford relief to the inhabitants.

One good work, however, which I do not care to leave hiding its light under a bushel, is the home for factory-girls, managed by the Sisters of St. John the Baptist, Clewer, and situated in Southwark.

Here, girls employed in the many factories of the neighbourhood during the day can, if they are willing to submit to the rules, find a real home for a small weekly payment, and escape the wretched and too often vicious surroundings of the places in which their parents live.

With a full knowledge of all the temptation which besets the work-girls who have to spend their leisure in these slums none can doubt the good work such institutions may do.

On the night of our visit we were conducted from basement to roof by one of the Sisters; we saw the girls and heard their histories from their own lips, and learnt how terrible was the sin and misery which had forced them to look upon their vile homes with loathing, and how fierce the temptation which beset them when left to themselves.

These girls are of the class which most deserve help; they work hard at dangerous trades for their living, and they pay for their food and board. What the charity does is to throw a certain home influence around them, give them cleanliness and godliness, and preserve them to some extent from the contamination of the streets - streets here which are thronged at night with the worst types of humanity the great city can show.

SISTER.

The story of the Mission is romantic. A lady Mrs. Hun was left a young widow. After less than two years of married life her husband died suddenly. She devoted herself to her own daughter, who grew up into a beautiful girl. The morning after her first ball the young lady was found dead in her bed. To assuage her grief and keep from breaking down utterly, the bereaved mother determined to devote herself to charity. The fearful condition of the young girls in this neighbourhood was brought to her attention, and with her fortune and her dead daughter's she devoted herself to establishing a home for factory-girls.

Such is the short and simple story of how this excellent institution was founded. How it is carried out, how the girls cling to the Home, and how thoroughly they appreciate its comforts, any lady can see who cares to take a trip as far as Union Street, Borough, and ring the bell of the All Hallows' Mission-House.

The work which these girls have to do in return for a small wage is generally of a dangerous character. Many of them literally snatch their food from the jaws of death.

One girl in the Home was white and ill and weak, and her story may be taken as a sample. She worked at the "bronzing," that is, a branch of the chromo-lithography business, and it consists in applying a fluid, which gives off a poisonous exhalation, to certain work. Bronzing enters largely into the composition of those Christmas pictures which delight us so much at the festive season, and which adorn the nursery of many a happy, rosy-checked English child.

The law recognising the dangerous nature of the works says that the girls doing it shall be allowed a pint of milk per day, the milk in some way counteracting the effect of the poison the girls inhale. It will hardly be believed that some of the best firms refuse to comply with the regulation and if the guts complain they are at once discharged.

Now, the wages paid are seven shillings per week. To keep at their employment it is necessary that the workers take castor-oil daily, and drink at least a pint of milk. They must either pay for these luxuries out of their scanty earnings or go without, and eventually find their way to the hospital.

Take another trade - the fur-pulling. The women and girls employed at this are in some shops locked in the room with their work, and have to eat their food there.

If you had ever seen a room crowded with girls pulling the fluff from cats, rabbits, rats, and goodness knows what other animals, you would appreciate the situation better. The fluff, the down, and the small hairs smother everything, and are necessarily swallowed by the occupants of the room with pernicious effect. Yet it is the custom of some of the men in the trade to force their employees to eat under such circumstances, that is, to swallow their food thickly coated with the hairs from which nothing can preserve it.

Why do not the women refuse? Because they would be discharged. There are always hundreds ready and eager to take their places. The struggle for bread is too fierce for the fighters to shrink from any torture in its attainment. With the dangers of the white-lead works, which employ a large number of these families, most people are now familiar; at least, those who read the inquests must be. In addition to the liability to lead-poisoning, in many of these works the machinery is highly dangerous. In spite of the Employer's Liability' Act, the victims of machinery accidents - that is, when they are women or children - rarely get compensation.

The hospitals are full of accidents from these causes often the negligence is that of a fellow-workman, but in at least half-a-dozen cases I have investigated not one shilling of compensation has the victim obtained.

RABBIT-PULLING.

Saw-mills, and places where steam and circular saws are used, employ a large number of boys. If you were to give a tea-patty to saw-mill boys, the thing that would astonish you would be the difficulty of finding half-a-dozen of your guests with the proper number of fingers.

I know one little lad who is employed at pulling out the planks which have been pushed through the machine by men, and he has one hand now on which only the thumb is left. Then there is the lemonade-bottling, which is another industry largely employing the lads of poor neighbourhoods. The bottles are liable to burst, and cases of maiming are almost of daily occurrence. The bottlers are obliged to wear masks to protect their faces, but their hands are bound to be exposed to the danger.

These are a few of the dangerous and unhealthy occupations by which the poor live, and I have enumerated those largely practised by children. I have done so show how little we can wonder if for lack of a protecting arm, or that parental love which is, alas, so rare a thing in the very poor districts, these boys and girls yield to the first temptation to go wrong, and instead of risking life and limb for a paltry wage, take to those paths of vice which we have it on the highest authority are always the most easy of access.

As we leave the home of the factory girls we come upon a scene which illustrates the life outside. A big crowd of foul-mouthed, blackguardly boys and girls, with a few men and women among them, are gathered round two girls who are fighting fiercely. They have quarrelled, a bystander tells us, in the adjacent public-house about a young man. He is considered her legitimate property by one lady, and the said lady has surprised him treating her rival to gin. Neither of the girls are more than seventeen, I should say, yet they are fighting and blaspheming and using words that make even myself and my collaborator shudder, used as we are by this time to the defiled Saxon of the slums.

"Go it, Sal," yells a female friend, and Sal goes it, and the boys and girls stand round and enjoy the spectacle, and add their chorus of blasphemy and indecency to the quarrel duet of the Madame Angots of the gutter

I had nearly forgotten an incident which occurred when we were in the factory-girls' home, and which is not without its lesson as showing the value even these girls attach to social position. One young lady was introduced to us as having a sweetheart who always brought her home of an evening with great punctuality. "What is your sweetheart? I asked. "A boot-finisher; was the answer. "Where does he work - at what firm? " "He works just by Fenchurch Street Station. "Is it a large bootmaker's?" "Well, it ain't exactly a bootmaker's; he's a shoeblack." I never heard a shoeblack called a boot-finisher before, but I think the euphemism was allowable in a young lady who wishes to exalt the commercial status of her intended.

I alluded in a recent Chapter to the costermongers as a large and worthy class. Since that Chapter was written I have explored a district which is almost exclusively inhabited by them - a portion of St. Luke's. To what I have already written let me add that until now I had not the slightest conception that things were so bad as they really are. My visit was early in the morning, before the men and women had gone out with their loads. If you could have seen the condition of the rooms and yards piled up with rotting vegetable refuse, and the way in which the cabbages and the fruit were stowed for the night, and where they were stowed, it would have cured such among you as are fond of a bargain at the door from ever patronising a barrow again.

Out of the fetid one room where man and wife and family slept they carried the stuff that their neighbours were to eat. It had passed the night with them, and the green-stuff was decidedly faded and languid. It was piled on the barrow, and then soused with dirty water, and so wheeled away to be cried up and down the streets of London.

No wonder diseases are spread if from such poisoned fever-breeding dens as this the food is carried with all its impurity day after day to be hawked from door to door!

I do not blame the costers. They must get where there is an open space for their barrows handy, some bit of waste land where houses have been condemned and pulled down. They stack their harrows here, taking off one wheel and carrying it home, that their property may not be wheeled off in the night. But areas with this waste land are limited, so up go the prices, and the coster must pay. In Green - Arbour Court, St. Luke's, I came upon a man who was paying eight shillings a week for one miserable room, and all round the district the very vilest accommodation fetches something very near that figure.

Eight shillings a week for one room! Surely a class that can pay that must be worth catering for even by the five per cent. philanthropists.

Some time ago there was a scheme to build a goods station in this district, and before the Bill could be considered Parliament required a labouring-class statement, that is, a statement of the number of poor people who would be displaced.

On looking through the figures I find that to build this station about 3,000 poor people would have to be turned out of their houses.

"FINE STRAW—B—RIES. FINE FRESH-GATHERED STRÆBUT—RIEES."

It is the pulling down of area after area for the purpose of building large warehouses and railway stations, and that sort of thing, which is, of course, at the root of the overcrowding. The accommodation becomes more limited year after year, and the property built as dwelling-houses under the Artisans' Dwelling Act does not, as I have pointed out before, offer any accommodation to the class displaced. In another district I made a discovery which I fancy must be unique. I found a public house which was a high way for traffic. You went out of a street into a bar - you walked straight through and found yourself in a network of courts behind. I found on inquiry that for years the public house had been used as a footpath, and I have no doubt it was found highly convenient by ladies and gentlemen in hurry to escape observation.

In another district still I unearthed as sweet a little story as any of the annals of jobbery can, I imagine, furnish. Let me tell it carefully, for the law of libel is a fearful and wonderful thing, and I have no desire to have the proprietors of this journal reading their next Christmas number in Holloway Gaol.

A big block of buildings falling into decay were for sale. A person officially connected with the parish drew the attention of the sanitary officers to them, and had them condemned as unfit for habitation. Directly this was done the parish gentleman, in conjunction with a firm of speculators, bought the property for a bagatelle - for old building material, in fact. But the new proprietors didn't pull it down - not they. They gave a coat of whitewash here and there, and let every single room again directly at increased rentals, and every single room is full of rent-payers now. The street of houses which was condemned five years ago has been a little gold mine, and a handsome fortune has been made out of it by the very people who insisted upon calling the attention of the sanitary authorities to it.

It is needless to say that the same attention has never been solicited since.

I should like to know how many more blocks of property - unfit for human habitation - are held in the same way in London.

I fancy the revelations on this subject would be startling to a degree.

Yet amidst all these horrors and sufferings, working at dangerous trades, housed in death-traps, neglected and persecuted, the poor manage to live, and some of them to amuse themselves. How they amuse themselves we shall shortly see.

CHAPTER X.

WHEN I come to the task of describing how the poor amuse themselves, there comes back to me the memory of a certain "exam" I submitted myself to in the happy long ago. I am not quite sure now whether the result was to be a clerkship in Somerset House, or a certificate of proficiency which I could frame, and glaze, and hang up in my bedroom ; all I remember is, that I was taken up to London with half-a-dozen of my fellow-collegians, and deposited in a large room, at a desk, and that in front of me was placed a paper with a string of printed questions on it, which I was requested to answer in writing. The questions were not particularly flabbergasting then, though I doubt whether I could answer a single one of them correctly now; but that which carried terror to my fluttering heart at once was the special note which enjoined me to write my answers briefly and concisely. There are certain questions which will not be answered in half-a-dozen words. Several such there were on my examination-paper, and such a question, after a lapse of years, again stands and defies me to mortal combat.

"How do the poor amuse themselves?"

The name of their amusements is legion, and to catalogue them briefly is beyond my powers, even after a long life passed among postcards, which are used on one side only, and telegraph forms, on which one word over twenty puts 25 per cent, on to the cost of transmission.

The principal amusement of the people who have no money is, I take it, loafing at street corners and gossiping with their neighbours, and the form of enjoyment by far the most prevalent is getting drunk.

The public-house, after centuries 6f philanthropic tall-talk and hundreds of miles of newspaper and magazine writing, tracts and essays, remains still the Elysian field for the tired toiler. The well-meaning efforts of the societies which have endeavoured to attract the poor to hear countesses play the fiddle and baronets sing comic songs in temperance halls have not been crowned with anything like success, for the simple reason that there is an air of charity and goody-goody about the scheme which the poor always regard with suspicion. They want their amusement as a right, not as a favour, and they decline to be patronised.

The public-house, then, is still the centre of attraction for the masses during their leisure-the public-house and its giant offspring, the music-hall. The old Free and Easy, held every Monday or every Saturday, as the case night be, in the bar-parlour or the big room up stairs, is dying the death - the halls have killed it. There are a few still in existence, but the attendance is meagre, and the entertainment is only kept up by ambitious amateurs of the type who sit back in a chair and close their eyes to sing a sentimental ballad, and the young gentlemen who are anxious to exchange the workshop or the counter for the footlights, and try their hand first at the comic songs of Messrs. Arthur Roberts and McDermott before the dozen or so of the bar-parlour frequenters of the Blue Bear who make up the weekly audiences of the "Free and Easy."

The old sporting-houses, once the resort of half the blackguardism of the East-end and a good deal of the West, have gone down before the steady bowling of the law. The friendly bouts with the gloves between local "chickens" and "novices," which once were regular Saturday night amusements, are few and far between, and dog-fights and ratting matches have to be searched for by the curious as diligently as though they were looking for a policeman in a suburban neighbourhood, and the result is generally the same.

That boxing and ratting, and other forms of the "fancy," still exist as part of the amusement of the lower orders, is perfectly true, but they exist in such a hole-and-corner, out-of-the-way, few-and-far-between style, that they can no longer be classed as among the amusements of those who cannot afford to pay high prices of admission to illegal entertainments.

The noble art of self-defence did undoubtedly linger among the lower orders as a pastime long after it had passed out of favour with the Corinthians, and many of the porters of Billingsgate, Covent Garden, and Smithfield, waterside labourers, costermongers, and street hawkers are to this day famous as "bruisers," and given to indulge their friends at odd times with a display of their prowess on the extreme Q.T., in quiet out-houes and secluded spots where the police are unlikely to mar the harmony of the proceed-ings. Such meetings, when they do take place, always attract a mob of the lowest riff-raff, and if there be, as is generally the case, a charge for admission, ragged wretches, who look as though a crust of bread and cheese would be of considerable advantage to them, manage in some mysterious way to find the requisite amount of silver, without the production of which the crystal Bar of the Pug's Paradise moves not, and the sporting Pen is sent disconsolate away.

"'ERE Y' ARE; THREE SHOTS A PENNY! NOW'S YER CHAANCE!!!"

It has been my good or evil fortune, in my desire to know all sorts and conditions of men, to witness some of the latest revivals of glove-fighting; now in drill-sheds, now in top floors of public-houses, and once in the upper floor of a workshop, which nearly gave way with the weight of accumulated blackguardism collected. These, it is only fair to say, were mostly "ramps," or swindles, got up to obtain the gate money, and generally interrupted by circumstances arranged beforehand by those who were going to "cut up" the plunder.

As a matter of fact, the suburban racecourse has now absorbed most of the poorer patrons of the ring, and the fighting men - that is, the class who are of the slum order - find employment in connection with the betting lists and booths. The turf is still as highly patronised as ever in poor districts, in spite of the objection of the police to ready-money betting, and the racing element enters largely into the recreations of the residuum.

This, however, is hardly the class of amusement with which we are concerned, which is more that which engages the attention of the poorer toilers after work hours. The Saturday night is the great night in these districts for the play which prevents Jack being dull, and accordingly it is a Saturday night we select to take a trip once more through the streets of the unfashionable quarters.

We choose the heart of a thickly-populated district, and emerge from comparative quiet into a Babel of sound. A sharp turn brings us from a side street into one long thoroughfare ablaze with light and as busy as a fair. It is a fair in fact; the pavement and the roadway are crowded with a seething mass of human beings side by side with the meat-stalls, the fish-stalls, the fruit and vegetable-stalls, and the cheap finery-stalls; there are shooting-galleries, try-your-strength machines, weighing-chairs, raffling-boards, and nothing is lacking but "three shies a penny "and a Richardson's show to make a complete picture of an old-fashioned fair.

All the world and his wife are out to-night, and the wildest extravagances are being committed in the way of fish for supper to-night and vegetables for dinner to-morrow. The good housewives, basket on arm, are giving the ready-witted hawker as much repartee over the price of a cabbage as would suffice for a modern comedy.

The workman, released from his toil, is smoking his pipe and listening open-mouthed to the benevolent and leather-lunged gentlemen who are sacrificing household utensils, boots, ornaments, concertinas, and cutlery, at prices which would have cajoled the money from the pocket of a Daniel Dancer. And the golden youth of the neigbbourhood, with their best attire on, all cut after one relentless fashion - the mashers of the East - they too are out in full force, entering into the wild delirium of reckless pleasure which the scene invites.

The principal amusement in the street, apart from buying knives and neckties of the Cheap Jack and entering into a raffle for a concertina, which is the sole business of one densely crowded stall, seems to be shooting at a target - three shots a penny, and the prize for hitting the bull's-eye, a real Whitechapel cigar. This seems to he an intensely popular pastime with the boys, and the one who wins a cigar and turns away and proudly lights it is at once surrounded by a crowd of lads, who praise his skill and plead for a puff at the luxury which his marksmanship has won for him.

AN EAST-END "MASHER."

The public-houses are crammed all along the line. This form of "amusement " seems to be the favourite one with families, for in house after house there are little groups comprising a grey-headed old lady with a glass of neat gin, a buxom young woman with a baby and ditto, and a burly young fellow with a big pewter. On barrels against the wall and on forms set round, these groups of young men and young women arc talking more or less loudly, and spending an idle hour in putting the bulk of the week's wages down their throats. It is a truism to say that the curse of the lower orders is drink, but no man with eyes can walk on a Saturday night through the homes of the wage-earning class without feeling how terrible the evil is, and how earnestly, without being either a bigot or a fanatic, every man who has a chance should raise his voice at the criminal neglect which flings these poor people into the arms of their only caterer - the publican.

A CRITICAL AUDIENCE ON THE HORIZON OF "PERE-DARAMS."

Many people object to the music-halls as sinks of iniquity. That they are unmixed blessings I am not going to contend, but if properly conducted they do an immense deal of comparative good. Drink is sold certainly in some of them, but few people get drunk. A very little liquour goes a long way at a hall, and the people being amused and interested in the entertainments do not want much liquid sustenance. The entertainment at some of the lower halls might, it is true, be weeded of certain suggestive songs, but after all the best patrons of indecency are the rich, and the poor give their loudest applause to skilful dancing and sentimental singing. A good ballad, well sung, "fetches" the masses as nothing else will, and they can appreciate good music. If the managers of the halls would do away with the coarser items in their programmes, I should say that this form of entertaining the masses was absolutely calculated to benefit them. I am quite certain that to keep young men and women off the streets and away from bars is no bad service to the cause of morality. In the east of London there are several places where a big entertainment is given and no liquor is sold at all. At one of them -

the best of its kind in London - there are two houses nightly. From seven till nine dramas are performed, then everybody is turned out and the house is refilled with a fresh audience for a music-hall entertainment - and nearly every evening the theatre is crammed to suffocation; the admission is 1d. the gallery, 2d. the pit, and 3d. and 6d. the upper circle and boxes. On the night of our visit there wasn't room to cram another boy in the place; the gallery and pit were full of boys and girls of from eight to fifteen, I should say, and the bulk of the audience in the other parts were quite young people.

WHY PAY A DOCTOR?

The gallery was a sight which once seen could never be forgotten. It was one dense mass of little faces and white bare arms twined and intertwined like snakes rotund a tree - tier above tier of boys rising right away from the front rows until the heads of the last row touched the ceiling. It was a jam - not a crowd-when one boy coughed it shook the thousands wedged in and rotund about; and when one boy got up to go out he had to crawl and walk over the heads of the others; space below for a human foot to rest there was absolutely none.

All this vast audience was purely local. Our advent, though our attire was a special get-up for the occasion, attracted instant attention, and the cry of " Hottentots" went round. " Hottentots "is the playful way in this district of designating a stranger, that is to say, a stranger, come from the West.

The entertainment was admirable; the artistes were clever, and in only one case absolutely vulgar; and the choruses were joined in by the entire assembled multitude.

When it was time for the chorus to leave off and the singer to go on again, an official in uniform, standing by the orchestra, and commanding the entire house, raised his hand, and instantly, as if by magic, the chorus ceased.

Of course there are disturbances, but the remedy is short and effective. Two young gentlemen in the dress circle fought and used bad language to each other. Quick as lightning the official was up stairs with a solitary policeman, the delinquents were seized by the collar, and, before they could expostulate, flung down a flight of steps and hustled out into the street with a celerity which could only come of constant practice.

It is fair to say that the youths seemed quite ready for the emergency, and took their "chucking out" most skilfully. I should have fallen and broken my nose had I been flung down a flight of steps like that; these youths were evidently prepared, and took a flying jump on to the landing. What they did outside I can't say, but after a chorus of hooting at the helmeted intruder, the audience resumed their seats, and the performance went on without any further interruption.

Such places as this - the cheaper halls, gaffs, and sing-songs - are the principal places of resort of the ladies and gentlemen of the slums who have coppers to spare for amusement. But the streets themselves offer to many a variety of entertainments for which there is no charge. A horse down is a great source of quiet enjoyment; a fight attracts hundreds; and round in one dark spot, we came upon an *al fresco* gambling establishment, where some hundreds of lads were watching half-a-dozen of their companions playing some game at cards on a rough deal stand, presided over by a villainous-looking Jew. What the game was we could not stay long enough to study, for our approach was signalled by scouts, and as we came close to the crowd it dispersed as if by magic, and the gentleman with the board produced from his pocket a quantity of coughdrops, and flung them upon the board, bawling aloud, "Six a penny, six a penny !" in a manner intended to convince us that this was his occupation. Possibly we were mistaken for plain clothes policemen ; at any rate, we were followed and watched for fully a hundred yards.

The mock-litany scoundrel had a big crowd in one street, and an infant phenomenon - a boy who played all the popular airs down the spout of a coffee-pot-was largely patronised; but the biggest audience of the evening surrounded a gentleman who, mounted on a cart, was at once carrying on the business of an ointment vendor and the profession of an improvisatore. His ointment was only a penny a box, but its intrinsic merits were priceless. It was warranted to draw glass or iron or steel from any part of the human body with one application; also to cure weak eyes, bad legs, and sores of all descriptions.

The gentleman indulged in anecdotes full of ancient and modern history, all proving the value of his ointment, and every now and then he dropped into rhyme.

> If you have a bad leg, and physicians have given you up,
> Or you've been to the doctor's who've half poisoned you
>   with nasty stuff,
> Perhaps you fancy that it's no good that your leg can't be cured;
> But Moore's ointment will do of that, rest assured.
> Try it ; if it don't succeed, you're only a penny the worse.
> If you don't try it, you may think of it too late, when you're

in your funeral hearse.

It's cured hundreds, and thousands will testify It is good for
even the tenderest baby's eye.

Why pay a doctor, or in hospital lie for months, When this
ointment will cure you by only applying it once?

Then the gentleman broke off into prose, and related how Napoleon,
in the Island of "Helber" had bought a box of this very ointment of
the seller's grandfather, who was under the British Government
then, and had declared, it ever he got free, every soldier in the
French army should have a box in his knapsack, and also gave
certain humorous reminiscences of his own struggles to get the
English people to believe in the specific. His eloquence was not
thrown away, for he did a roaring trade, and at one time a perfect
forest of hands was held. up to secure the famous ointment.

The crowd thins as closing time comes, and the hawkers pack up
what is left of their stock, strike their naptha-lamps, and wheel off
the ground. What they have left they will sell in the early market on
Sunday morning.

CHAPTER XI.

OOKING over what I have written I am struck by what seems to me an important omission. In driving home the nail of the miserable condition in which the poor are forced to live, I have perhaps led the reader to imagine that the better instincts of humanity have been utterly stamped out - that the courts and alleys are great wastes of weed, where never a flower grows.

I should be loth to father such an idea as this. In the course of many years of the closest contact with the most poverty-stricken of our fellow-men, I have learnt to think better, and not worse, of human nature, and- to know that love, self-sacrifice, and devotion flourish in this barren soil as well as in the carefully-guarded family circles which are, or should be, forcing-houses for all that is choicest and most beautiful among human instincts.

Braver than many a hero who comes back from foreign plains with a deed of prowess to his credit and a medal on his breast, are some of the ragged rank and file who fight the battle of life against overwhelming odds, and never flinch or falter, but fight on to the end; and the end, alas is rarely victory or renown-too often the guerdon of these brave soldiers is the workhouse, the hospital, or a miserable death from cold and slow starvation, in a quiet corner of the street, where they have sunk down to rise no more.

It is often a matter of wonder - at least I hope it is - to the good folks who skim their newspapers at the morning meal and take their politics, their Court Circular, and their police intelligence at a single draught between their sips of coffee, what becomes of the children whose fathers and mothers are sent to prison for long or short periods.

The State does not consider the innocent victims of crime; the law punishes the individual without taking thought of the consequences to those who may be dependent upon her or him for bread. I am not advocating any leniency to a culprit on the score of his value as a breadwinner; I am simply going to state a few facts, and leave my readers to draw any moral they please from the narrative.

Half the men and women of the lower orders who are imprisoned for various small offences, such as being drunk and incapable, assaulting each other, or committing petty larceny, are married and have families. Bachelors and spinsters are rare after a certain age in low neighbourhoods, and large families are invariably the result of early marriages, or that connection which, among the criminal classes and the lowest grade of labourers, does duty for the legally-solemnised institution.

"I'LL DO FOR YOU WEN I COME OUT."

Many persons who wander into police-courts at the East-end, either for business or amusement, must be familiar with the poor woman, a baby in her arms, and her head strapped up with sticking-plaster and surgical bandages, who begs the magistrate not to punish the hulking fellow in the dock who has so brutally ill-used her. The woman knows, what the magistrate and the public ignore, that the three months' sentence means comfort and luxury to the man - misery and starvation to the woman and her little ones.

He has probably been the chief bread-winner; the woman is incapacitated by his ill-treatment from doing any work, and so she and her children are suddenly rendered penniless and homeless. She must crawl back from the court to her miserable garret, and when her babies ask for food pawn her few rags to get it for them ; and when all is pawned and gone, she cannot pay her nightly rent, so she must turn out with her little family into the streets or go into the work house. Such a case we heard as we looked into a police court on our travels ; and 1 shall not soon forget the agonised cry of the woman as the magistrate gave her husband six-months, and congratulated her on being temporarily rid of such a ruffian.

"Great God, what will become of us now?"

"IT'S ALL A MISTAKE, YOUR WUSHIP, ALL A MISTAKE ; HE DIDN'T DO NUFFINK, SIR WOULDN'T 'URT A FLY !"

I see that many humane people are asking what can be done to alleviate the sufferings of the poor. I don't know whether there is any society which looks after the wives and children of malefactors, and lends them a helping hand, if they deserve it, to tide over the absence of their sole source of income; but if there is not, I fancy here is work for idle hands to do, and a source for charity that, worked with discrimination and care, might alleviate one of the crushing evils to which poor families are liable. But these people are not always friendless, and it is a~ case I wish to quote which has led me to touch upon the subject.

In one wretched room we visited there were six little cues home at the mid-day hour from school.

"You have six children? " I said to the woman.

No, sir, only four; these two little ones ain't mine - they are staying with us."

I imagined that they were the children of a relative, and questioned the woman further, wondering how she cared. to i crowd her little den with extra visitors, and then the story came out.

These two extra mouths the good soul was feeding belonged to two little children whose mother, a widow, lived in a room above. For an assault upon the police she had been sent to prison. Thus the position of these orphans with a living parent was terrible. They would have been starved or taken to the workhouse, but this good creature went up and fetched them down to be with her own children, and made them welcome; she washed them and dressed them, and did for them all she could, and she intended to keep them if she was able till the mother came out.

"She didn't see that she had done anything wonderful It was only neighbourly-like, and my heart bled to see the poor young uns a-cryin', and that wretched and neglected and dirty."

Such cases as this are common enough - the true charity the charity which robs itself to give to others, is nowhere so common as among the poor. The widow's mite that won the Saviour's praise is cast into the great treasury daily, and surely stands, now, as then, far higher on the roll of good deeds than all the gold flung carelessly by the hands of the rich to every box rattler who promises "that the amount shall be duly acknowledged in the Times."

I will quote one more case, which has just come und my personal observation, and which illustrates the brave struggles against adversity of which those people are capable.

Our attention was directed to the circumstance by the head-mistress of the school which the children were attending, and who had noticed that they who had always been the cleanest and tidiest in the class were beginning to show signs of a little less motherly care. The children said their mother was too ill to do much, and we went to see her.

Mrs. B. had some children of her own, and in addition she and her husband had taken in a little girl whose father had gone off tramping in search of work.

We found her propped up in a chair looking terribly ill but in front of her in another chair was the wash-tub, and the poor woman was making a feeble effort to wash and wring out some of the children's things. She was dying. She was suffering from dropsy, and had not lain down for month - the water was rising rapidly and would soon reach her heart and kill her. Yet here she sat, scarcely able to breathe, and enduring untold agony, but making an effort to the very last to work and keep her little ones clean and tidy.

It is a glorious lot in life - these people's, is it no ? - to toil on and struggle, to resist temptation, and giving their youth and age to the hardest labour for a wage that barely staves off starvation, to know that when illness comes or time steals their strength away, they are mere burthens, refuse to be got rid of since it encumbers the land.

Can one blame them if, knowing their hard lot and the little reward the most virtuous life can bring them, they sink into the temptations spread around them? Remember, that for half their miseries, half their illness and premature decay, and much of the disease which cripples and carries off their children, the shameful way in which they arehoused, and the callous neglect of their rights as citizens by the governing class is responsible.

They are handicapped in the race from start to finish. And under these circumstances, such charity, such humanity, and such patience and long-suffering as exist among them are indeed worthy of admiration.

The natural instinct of man is to evil, and and when I read in little tracts and clerical addresses of the awful depravity of the "heathen in our midst," I am tempted to ask what the reverend gentlemen and shocked philanthropists expect. I say, with a full knowledge of their surroundings, that the lower classes of our great cities are entitled to the highest credit for not being twenty times more depraved than they are.

"I CAN SEE THAT THERE LITTLE GIT OF MY 'EM."

They are a class which contains the germs of all that goes to make up good citizenship, and the best proof of it is the patience with which they endure the systematic neglect of their more fortunate fellow-countrymen. In any other land but ours, the mighty mass of helots would long ago have broken their bonds and swept over the land in vast revolutionary hordes. They did not always know their power and had not enough knowledge to appreciate their wrongs. Education is opening their eyes, and their lips will be slow to express their new-born sentiments. It will be well to meet that movement half-way and yield to them that reform and humane recognition which some day they may all too noisily demand.

Here I am up on a platform and thumping away at the table and spouting what I have no doubt many excellent persons will think is rank communism, though it is nothing of the sort. *Peccari*, I apologise. The fumes of the misery I have passed through the last two months have got into my head and made me talk wildly. Let me resume my labour more in the character of a missionary or specialcorrespondent, and leave oratory and denunciation to the Sunday morning Wilkeses of Battersea Park.

We have no business out of doors at all - let us study another domestic interior. The scene, a street which lies cheek by jowl with the quarter where the world of fashion rolls nightly in comfortable carriages to enjoy theatrical and operatic performance in half-guinea stalls and three-guinea boxes, and where fabulous fortunes are made by those who can make Mr. and Mrs. Dives weep at imaginary woes or laugh at a merry jest or comic antic.

From such a scene as I am going to ask you to witness, thousands who crowd a theatre nightly to see a woman's head battered out against a sofa or a young man suffocate himself with the fumes of charcoal, would shrink back in disgust. But you will not, for if you have gone so far with us as this journey, you are, I feel sure, convinced that no good can come of hiding the worst phase of a question which is only dragged forward here that it may, by the very horror of its surroundings, arrest attention and so secure that discussion which must always precede a great scheme of reformation.

Come with me to this place. Our way lies through Clare Market, so don't go alone, for it is a dangerous neighbourhood to strangers. Come with me through strange sights and sounds, past draggled, tipsy women crowding the footway, and hulking fellows whose blasphemies fill the tainted air, pick your way carefully through the garbage and filth that litter the streets, and stop in this narrow thoroughfare which is but a stone's throw from many a stage that holds the mirror up to nature, and yet would shrink from holding such a scene as this.

We have stopped at a marine-store shop - we enter the passage and find our way up to the third floor. Here in a single room live a man, his wife, and three children. There has been an inquest on a baby who has died - poisoned by the awful atmosphere it breathed. We have stumbled up the dark crazy staircase at the risk of our limbs, to see this room in which the family live and sleep and eat, because in its way it is a curiosity. It has been the scene of an incident which one would hardly believe possible in this Christian country. For days in this foul room the body of a dead baby had to lie because the parish had no mortuary. Not only did the corpse have to lie here for days among the living, but on that little, table, propped against the window, the surgeon had to perform a post-mortem examination.

Think of it, you who cry out that the sufferings of these people are sensationally exaggerated-the dead baby was cut open in the one room where the mother and the other little ones, its brothers and sisters, lived and ate and slept. And why?

Because the parish had no mortuary, and no room in which post-mortems could be performed.

The jurymen who went to view the body sickened at the frightful exhalations of this death-trap, and one who had thirty years' experience of London said never had he seen a fouler den.

I have turned to the newspapers for a report of the inquest and found it, and I think it will be better to present it word for word. it is an ordinary newspaper report of what has happened and been legally investigated, and may carry conviction where my own unsupported testimony would fail.

"A coroner's inquiry was held last night by Mr. Langham, regarding the death of an infant aged two and a half months, the daughter of a butcher named Kent, who, with his wife and three children, occupy a single room on the third floor of premises used as a marine store in Wych Street. The inquiry was held in the Vestry Room of the parish. On the return of the jury from viewing the body - which lay in the room occupied by the family - one of the jurymen addressed the

112

coroner. He had, he stated, during his thirty years' residence in the parish, seen many places which he regarded as unfit for dwelling houses, but never had he seen one so bad as that which the jury had just visited. The staircase was dark and out of repair. The atmosphere inside was intolerable. Indeed, it was so bad that several of his fellow jurymen had felt ill while they were there. They hoped that this expression of opinion would have some effect in inducing the proper authorities to provide a mortuary for the district, and that families who lived in one room might not be compelled to sleep and take their meals with a dead body within sight. Mr. Samuel Mills, surgeon, 3, Southampton Street, Strand, medical officer to the Bow Street Division of Police, deposed that he had made a post-mortem examination of the body on a propped-up table placed in front of the window of the room occupied by the family. The cause of death was consumption of the brain. From the state of the atmosphere in which the child was born, it was unhealthy. Another child had died from the same cause. He thought the local authority ought to provide a mortuary, and also a room in which post-mortem examinations could be conducted. A verdict in accordance with the medical evidence was returned by the jury, who further expressed their opinion that the want of a mortuary was calculated to be detrimental to the health of the persons living in the district; that there being no mortuary was a disgrace to the local authority; and that the circumstances surrounding the case they had investigated were a disgrace to this enlightened age."

I will not add a word. I leave the newspaper report to arouse whatever thoughts it may in the minds of those who will peruse it. It is at least a revelation to many of "How the Poor Live."

Let me hark back again to the lighter side of my subject. I began the chapter with a story of the self-sacrifice of the poor. I will now end it with a little incident of which I was an eye-witness this week. Some poor children of the slums had "a day in the country given them" by a friend, at which I had the privilege of being present.

At tea, to every little one there were given two large slices of cake; I noticed one little boy take his, break a little piece oft eat it, and quietly secrete the remainder in his jacket pocket. Curious, and half suspecting what his intention was, I followed the lad when tea was over, to the fields.

"Eaten your cake yet?" I said.

"No, sir," he answered, colouring as though he had done something wrong.

"What are you going to do with it?"

"Please sir," he stammered, "I'm goin' to take it 'ome to mother. She's ill and can't eat nothink, and I thought as she might manage cake, sir."

In the train that brought those youngsters down came one white-faced child, who looked faint and ill with the walk to the station.

The head teacher, who has the history of child at her fingers' end, saw what was the matter.

"Had no breakfast to-day, Annie?"

No, ma'am," was the faltering reply.

There was a crowd of poor mothers at the station come to see the children off. One went out and presently returned with a penny, which she pressed into the child's hand - to buy herself something with. The woman had pawned her shawl for a copper or two in sheer womanly sympathy. Had she had the money about her she needn't have left the station.

There was a good deal of pawning that morning, I know, from an eye-witness, and all to give the little children a copper or two to spend.

And what a struggle there had been to get them something decent to wear for that grand day out If all the stories were written that could be told of the privations and sacrifices endured by mothers, that Sally and Jane and Will might look respectable at the treat, your heart would ache. As I don't wish it to, we will not go into the matter.

CHAPTER XII.

To get an odd job at the Docks is often the last hope of the labouring men who are out of regular employment, and to whom the acquisition of a few shillings for rent, and the means of subsistence for themselves and families, is a task fraught with as much difficulty as were some of the labours, the accomplishment of which added in no inconsiderable degree to the posthumous fame of Hercules.

When it is borne in mind that sometimes at the West India Docks - taking one for example - as many as 2,500 hands can be taken on in the morning, it will be easily understood that the chance of employment draws an immense concourse of men daily to the gates.

The time to see what I venture to think is one of the most remarkable sights in the world, is an hour at which the general public is not likely to be passing by.

Sometimes the hands are engaged as early as four, but it is generally about six o'clock that the quay-gangers ascend the rostrums or elevated stands which are placed all along the outside wall, and survey the huge crowd in front of them, and commence to call them out for work and send them into the different docks where the good ships lie, with their vast cargoes, waiting for willing hands to unload them.

The pay is fivepence an hour, and the day's work lasts for eight hours. It is miscellaneous, and a man is expected to put his hand to anything in the shape of loading or unloading that the occasion may require.

Stand outside the dock gates any morning about six, and you will have plenty to study among the vast crowd of met more or less dilapidated and hungry-looking who fill all the approaches and line the banks in front of the rostrums.

Many of them are regular men, who are called "Royals" and who are pretty sure to be taken on, their names being on the ganger's list and called out by him as a matter of course. These men show signs of regular employment, and differ very little from the ordinary labourer. The strangest part of the crowd are the ragged, wretched, wobegone-looking outcasts who are penniless, and whose last hope is that they may have the luck to be selected by the ganger. Many of these come from the distant parts of London, from the North, and the South, and the East, and the West.

Some of them have tramped all night, and flung themselves down to sleep at the great dock gates in the early dawn, determined to be in the front rank.

They are of all sorts, sizes, and conditions. Among them is the seedy clerk, the broken-down betting-man, the discharged soldier, the dismissed policeman, the ticket-of-leave man, the Jack-of-all-trades, the countryman, and the London rough. An enormous proportion of the regular men are Irish and of the ordinary labouring class, but now and then a foreigner or a neg ro crops up among the crowd. One man there is among them who wears his rough jacket and his old battered billycock with a certain air of gentility, and whose features are strangely refinecd when compared with the coarser lineaments of those around him.

In the Docks they call him "the nobleman." He is a gentleman by birth and education; he can swear, I believe, in four languages ; and as a matter of fact is the son of a baronet, and has a right to be called "sir" if be chose to demand it. Into the sad story which has brought about this social wreck it is no business of mine to enter, though to the friendly Dock police and to the gangers the baronet is ready enough it to tell it.

"ALL SORTS AND CONDITIONS OF MEN."

The baronet can work, in spite of his pedigree, as well as any of his mates, and the fivepence an hour is a god-send to him. Strange are the stories of vicissitude which many of these men can tell. I have said it is the last haven of the outcast, and by that I do not mean to imply that all dock labourers are destitute, but that among the huge crowd of outsiders who come daily to take their chance are many of those who form the absolutely most helpless and most hopeless of the London poor. No character is required for the work, no questions are asked; a man can call himself any name he likes so long as he has two hands and is willing to use them, that is all the Dock Company require. Among these men are hundreds of those whose cases are so difficult to deal with in respect of house accommodation. They are the men who have to pay exorbitant rents for the filthy single rooms of the slums, and whose fight with starvation is daily and hourly. They are the men earning precarious livelihoods who are objected to by the managers of all the new Industrial Dwellings, which have swept away acres of accommodation of an inferior class. A man who is a Dock labourer may earn a pound a week - he may earn only five shillings. Sometimes they get taken on every day in a week, and then for a fortnight they may have to go empty-handed from the gates day after day.

Once fix on your mind the wear and tear, the anxiety and doubt, the strain and harass, the ups and downs of a life like this, count the smallness of the gain and the uncertainty of employment, and you will understand why it is that the common body of men who are classed as "Dock labourers" are reckoned as among the poorest of the London poor who make an honest effort to keep out of the workhouse. Watch this crowd - there must be over two thousand present in the great outer circle. The gangers are getting into the rostrums - two tea ships have come in, and a large number of men will be required. Hope is on many faces now; the men who have been lying in hundreds sleeping on the bank opposite - so usual a bed that the grass is worn away - leap to their feet. The crowd surges close together, and every eye is fixed in the direction of the ganger, who, up in his pulpit, his big book with the list of the names of regular ten, or " Royals," open before him, surveys the scene and prepares for business. He calls out name after name, the men go up and take a pass, present it to the police at the gate, and file in to be told off to the different vessels. It is when the "Royals " are exhausted that the real excitement begins. The men who are left are over a thousand strong - they have come on the chance. The ganger eyes them with a quick, searching glance, then points his finger to them, "You - and you - and you - and you." The extra ten go thorough the usual formality and pass in. There is still hope for hundreds of them. The ganger keeps on engaging men - but presently he stops.

You can almost hear a sigh run through the ragged crowd. There comes into some of the pale, pinched faces a look of unutterable woe - the hope that welled up in the heart has sunk back again. There is no chance now. All the men wanted are engaged.

As you turn and look at these men and study them, these the unfortunate ones, you picture to yourself what the situation means to some of them. What are their thoughts as they turn away? Some of them perhaps have grown callous to suffering, hardened in despair. To-day's story is but the story of yesterday and will be the story of to-morrow. There is on many of their faces that look of vacant unconcern to everything that comes of long familiarity with adversity. They have the look of the man who came into the French Court of Justice to take his trial for murdering his colleague at the galleys, and who had branded on his arm his name. "Never a chance." Never a chance when a man gets that branded not on his arm but on his heart He takes bad luck very quietly. It is the good luck which would astonish and upset him.

Some of the men, new comers most of these, and not used to the game yet, show a certain rough emotion. it is fair to say it generally takes the form of an expletive. Others, men who look as though they had sunk by degrees from better positions, go away with a quivering lip and a flush of disappointment. If we could follow the thoughts of some of them, we should see far away and perhaps where in some wretched room a wife and children sit cowering and shivering, waiting for the evening to come, when father will bring back the price of the day's work he has gone to seek. it must be with a heavy heart that his wife towards midday hears the sound of her husband's footsteps on the creaking stairs. This advent means no joy to her. That footstep tells its sad, cruel tale in one single creak. He has not been taken on at the Docks - another weary day of despair has to be sat through, another night she and the little ones must go hungry to bed.

It must not be imagined that the men clear away directly who have not been engaged. Hope springs eternal in the human breast, and dozens of men still wait on in hope. It sometimes happens that a ship comes in late, or something happens, and more men are required. Then the ganger comes out and picks them from among the remaining crowd.

Dozens of them hang about on the off-chance until two; after that it rarely happens any men are engaged, so the last brave few who have stood with wistful eyes for six or eight hours at the gate, turn slowly on their heels and go - God knows where.

Some of them, I believe, are absolutely homeless and friendless, and hang about street corners, getting perhaps a bit of tobacco from one or another more fortunate in this world's goods than themselves, and with it stave off the gnawing pangs of hunger. They hang about up side streets and round corners till night comes, then fling themselves down and sleep where they can, and go back once more at dawn to the gates of their paradise, to wait and hope, and be disappointed perhaps again.

This is the dark side of the Dock labourer's story. It has a brighter and better one inside, where on miles and miles of wharf hundreds of men, package and bale-laden, are hurrying to and fro, stowing the produce of the world in shed after shed. Thousands of barrels of sugar are lying in one, and the air is perfectly sweet with it. The ground is treacly with it, and one's boots are saturated with it as one walks through a thick slime of what looks toffee gone wrong in a sweetstuff window on a hot summer day. Thousands of boxes of tea, just in from China are in another shed and their next door neighbours are myriads of bags of wheat. The steam cranes are going as far as the eye can see, whirling, and dragging, and swinging huge bale after bale greedily from the good ship's hold; lighters laden to the top are being piled higher still; whole regiments of men bent with precious burthens are filing from wharf to warehouse; the iron wheels of the trolley, as it is pushed rapidly over the asphalted floor, makes a music of its own; and the whole scene shut in with a background of shipping-argosies freighted with the wealth of the

Indies, the produce of many a land beyond the seas;- all this goes to make up a picture of industry and enterprise and wealth, which gives just a little pardonable pride to the Englishman who contemplates it for the first time.

The system in the Docks is admirable. The strange men who are taken on are not taken entirely on trust. There is a uniform scale of pay for old hands and new, but there is an overlooker to see that all work well. If a man shirks or makes himself in any way objectionable, the process is short and summary: "Go to the office and take your money." The man is discharged-he is paid for the time he has worked, but no more; and he can leave the Docks out of the question as a field for his talents, if he has shown himself a duffer. A mark is put against his name on the ganger's book.

At the door every man who leaves the Docks is searched. This is more of a preventive measure than anything else. The men handle many packages of valuable commodities which have been broken in transit, and could easily extract some for their private use.

It would not be hard for a gentleman brought face to face with a broken chest of tea to fill his pockets with loose pound or two, for instance. The search at the gate stops that. Knowing that detection is certain, those men who would be dishonest if they could get a chance see the impossibility of escaping with their plunder, and so, making a virtue of necessity, respect the eighth commandment. The Docks are in the custody of a special body of Dock police, who maintain order, keep guard night and day over the goods on the warehouse, search the men, and check all the carts and vans passing out or in at the gates, and are generally responsible for everything.

The boys employed as messengers between the Dock House in Billiter Street and the Docks themselves, and also the lads employed on the spot, are all dressed in a remark ably neat uniform, and add to the picturesqueness of the busy scene. All these boys are drilled, and come to attention and salute their superiors with the precision of old soldiers

I have given a little space to the inside of the Docks because such numbers of the men whose homes we have visited in previous chapters are employed there, and it is there that unskilled labour finds the readiest market.

But it is outside that one must search for the misery which those who know them best acknowledge to be the commonest lot of the Dock labourer.

Inside, when the men are at work, the beer barrel on a stand with wheels is trundled merrily along at certain hours, and there is a contractor who supplies the men with food. It is outside that the beer barrel and the food contractor find their occupation gone.

DOCK MESSENGER.

Poverty in its grimest form exists here, and it is for these men, struggling so bravely and waiting so patiently for the work their hands are only too willing to do, that philanthropists might look a little more earnestly into the question of house accommodation. Looking at the uncertainty of employment, it is not hard for any one to see that a rent of five shillings for a single room is too much for these men to pay, and they cannot go out into the suburbs, where rents are cheaper, because they could not get to the Docks in anything like condition to work.

These men must live within a reasonable distance of their labour, and to do so they have to pay exorbitant prices for vile accommodation. They are kept in the lowest depths of poverty, because rent almost exhausts all the money - all that the luckiest can hope to earn.

Honest sweat, the poet has told us, is a very noble decoration to a man's brow, and these men are plentifully decorated before their task is over, I can assure you. It is scandalous that having done all they can, .risked life and limb (for dock accidents are numerous and keep a hospital busy), and done their duty in that state of life to which it has pleased God to call them, they should have to creep home to fever dens and pestilential cellars - half the money they pay ought to go for food for themselves and their children, instead of into the well-lined pockets of those who are making fortunes out of the death-traps they call House Property.

This short and hurried sketch of life in the Docks is necessarily incomplete. Its one great feature connected with the subject of these articles my readers can see for themselves at any time they like to take a long walk in the very early morning. No one who does not see the vast crowd can appreciate the character and pathetic elements it contains. I cannot write them with my pen, nor can my collaborator draw them with his pencil.

But we can both of us gratefully acknowledge our indebtedness to Mr. A. T. A. Brownlow, of the London Offices, and Captain Sheppy, of the Dock Police, whose kindness enabled us to see under peculiar advantages this phase of

"HOW THE POOR LIVE."

CHAPTER XIII.

WITH the present chapter I bring this series of Papers to a close. I have endeavoured briefly to present to the reader a few of the phases of existence through which their poorer brethren pass. I have necessarily left untrodden whole acres of ground over which a traveller in search of startling revelations might with advantage have journeyed. But startling revelations were not the objects I and my collaborator had in view when we undertook these sketches. Our object was to skim the surface lightly, but sufficiently to awaken in the general mind an interest in one of the great social problems of the day. A few of the evils of the present system of overcrowding and neglected sanitation, I have the courage to believe, have been brought home for the first time to a world of readers outside the hitherto narrow circle of philanthropists who take an active interest in the social condition of the masses.

One word with regard to the many letters which have appeared in the *Pictorial World,* and which have reached us privately. There seems a very general and a very earnest desire among the writers to do something for the people on whose behalf we have appealed to their sympathy.

While fully appreciating the kind-heartedness and the generous feelings evoked, I cannot help regretting that in too many instances the idea prevails that charity can ameliorate the evils complained of. I have been grievously misunderstood if anything I have said has led to the belief that all Englishmen have to do to help the denizens of the slums and alleys is to put their hands in and pull out a sovereign or a shilling.

It is legislation that is wanted, not almsgiving. It is not a temporary relief, but a permanent one, that can alone affect, in any appreciable manner, the condition of the one-roomed portion of the population of great cities.

Charity is to be honoured wherever it is found, but charity unless accompanied by something else, may do more evil than good. There are in London scores and scores of men and women who live by getting up bogus charities and sham schemes for the relief of the poor. Hundreds of thousands of pounds pass annually through the hands of men whose antecedents, were they known, would make a careful householder nervous about asking them into his hall if there were any coats and umbrellas about.

I am not a thick and thin supporter of the C.O.S. At various times I have been bitterly opposed, both to its theories and its practices; but it certainly has done an immense deal of good in exposing some of the scoundrels who appeal to the best sympathies of human nature under absolutely false pretences.

It is not so long ago that a man who had been convicted of fraud was found the flourishing proprietor of a mission to the poor, or something of the sort, and whose annual income for two years past had been over a couple of thousand pounds, against an expenditure in tracts, rent, and blankets of one hundred and thirty-six pounds.

In another instance, the promoter of a charity which had been in a flourishing condition for years, actually had his villa at St. John's Wood, and kept his brougham - his total source of income being the charity itself.

If I quote these cases here it is not to hinder the flow of the broad, pure stream of charity by one single obstacle, but to show such of my readers as may need the hint how dangerous and delusive it is to think that careless alms-giving is in any shape or form a real assistance to the poor and suffering.

People who wish to do good must give their time as well as their money. They must personally investigate all those cases they wish to relieve, and they must set about seeing how the causes which lead to misery and suffering can be removed.

How are the evils of overcrowding-how are the present miseries of the poor to be removed-in what way can the social status of the labouring classes be permanently raised? Not by collecting-cards or funds, not by tracts or missions, but by remedial legislation - by State help and State protection, and by the general recognition of those rights of citizenship which should be as carefully guarded for the lowest class as for the highest

We live in a country which practically protects the poor and oppressed of every land under the sun at the expense of its own. We organise great military expeditions, we pour out blood and money *ab libitum* in order to raise the social condition of black men and brown - the woes of an Egyptian, or a Bulgarian, or a Zulu, send a thrill of indignation through honest John Bull's veins. and yet at his very door there is a race so oppressed, so hampered, so utterly neglected, that its condition has become a national scandal.

A SKETCH FROM LIFE

Is it not time that the long-promised era of domestic legislation gave some faint streaks of dawn in the parliamentary sky? Are we to wait for a revolution before we rescue the poor from the clutches of their oppressors? are we to wait for the cholera or the plague before we remedy a condition of things which sanitarily is without parallel civilised countries?

There is a penalty for packing cattle too closely together - why should there be none for improperly packing men and women and children? The law says that no child shall grow up without reading, writing, and arithmetic; but the law does nothing that children may have air, and light, and shelter.

No one urges that the State should be a grandmother to the citizens, but it should certainly exercise ordinary parental care over its family.

To quote an instance of the gross neglect of the interests of the poor by the State, take the working of the Artisans' Dwelling Act. Space after space has been cleared under the provision of this Act, thousands upon thousands of families have been rendered homeless by the demolition of whole acres of the slums where they hid their heads, and in scores of instances the work of improvement has stopped with the pulling down. To this day the cleared spaces stand empty - a cemetery for cats, a last resting-place for worn-out boots and tea-kettles. The consequence of this is, that the hardships of the displaced families have been increased a hundredfold. So limited is now the accommodation for the class whose wage-earning power is of the smallest, that in the few quarters left open to them, rents have gone up too per cent, in five years - a room which once let for 2s. a week is now 4s. Worse even than this, the limited accommodation has left the renters helpless victims of any extortion or neglect the landlords of these places may choose to practise.

The tenants cannot now ask for repairs, for a decent water supply, or for the slightest boon in the way of Improvement. They must put up with dirt, and filth, and putrefaction-with dripping walls and broken windows, with all the nameless abominations of an unsanitary hovel, because if they complain the landlord can turn them out at once, and find dozens of people eager to take their places who will be less fastidious. It is Hobson's choice - that shelter or none - and it is small wonder that few families are stoical enough to move from a death-trap to a ditch or a doorstep for the sake of a little fresh air. The law which allows them the death-trap denies them the doorstep - that is a property which must not be overcrowded.

Now, is it too much to ask that in the intervals of civilizing the Zulu and improving the condition of the Egyptian fellah the Government will turn its attention to the poor of London and see if in its wisdom it cannot devise a scheme to remedy this terrible state of things ?

The social, moral, and physical improvement of the labouring classes is surely a question as important say as the condition of the traffic at Hyde Park Corner, or the disfigurement of the Thames Embankment. If one-tenth of the indignation which burst forth when a ventilator ventured to emit a puff of smoke on the great riverside promenade to the injury of the geraniums in Temple Gardens could only be aroused over the wholesale stifling and poisoning of the poor which now goes on all over London, the first step towards a better state of things would have been taken.

Why does that indignation find no stronger outlet than an occasional whisper, a nod of the head, a stray leading article, or a casual question in the House sandwiched between an inquiry concerning the Duke of Wellington's statue and one about the cost of cabbage-seed for the kitchen-garden at Buckinghmam Palace ?

The answer probably will be, that up to a recent date the magnitude of the evil has not been brought home to the general public or the members of the legislature. M.P.'s do not drive through the Mint or Whitechapel, nor do they take their constitutional in the back slums of Westininster and Drury Lane. What the eye does not see the heart does not grieve after, and the conservative spirit born and bred in Englishmen makes them loth to start a crusade against any system of wrong until its victims have begun to start a crusade of their own, to demonstrate in Trafalgar Square, and to hold meetings in Hyde Park. There is a disposition in this country not to know that a dog is hungry till it growls, and it is only when it goes from growling to snarling, and from snarling to sniffing viciously in the vicinity of somebody's leg, that the somebody thinks it time to send out a flag of truce in the shape of a bone. We don't want to wait until the dog shows its teeth to know that he has such things. We want the bone to be offered now - a good marrowy bone with plenty of legislative meat upon it. He has been a good, patient, long-suffering dog, chained to a filthy kennel for years, and denied even a drink of clean water, let alone a bone, so that the tardy offering is at least deserved.

It would be easy to show how the amelioration of the condition of the lower classes would be beneficial to the entire community, but it is scarcely worth while to put the question on such low grounds. The boon craved should come as an act of justice, not as a concession wrung from unwilling hands by fear, or granted with interested motives.

Briefly, and narrowing the question down to its smallest dimensions, what is wanted is this. The immediate erection on cleared spaces of tenements suitable to the classes dislodged. A system of inspection which would not only cause the demolition of unhealthy houses, but prevent unhealthy houses being erected - a certain space should be insisted on for every human being inhabiting a room - say 300 cubic feet for each person, and this regulation should be enforced by inspection of labouring-class dwellings, the enforcement of proper sanitary regulations, and a higher penalty for any breach of them ; the providing of increased bath and washing accommodation in every crowded district; - the erection of proper mortuaries in every parish, and the preservation in every district of certain open spaces to act as lungs to the neighbourhood - all these should be items in any remedial scheme. Beyond this, the poor should be encouraged in every possible way to decentralise. They must at present all crowd round the big centres of employment, because the means of travelling to and fro are beyond the reach of their slender purses. But if a system of cheap conveyance by tram or rail for the working-classes could be developed, they would scatter themselves more and more about the suburbs, and by their own action reduce the exorbitant rents they are now called upon to pay.

Again, there should be in all new blocks of tenements built for this class accommodation for the hawkers and others who have barrows which they must put somewhere, and who are compelled at times to house the vegetable and animal matter in which they deal. A man who sells cabbages in the streets cannot leave his unsold stock to take care of itself at night, so he takes it home with him. At present he and his family generally sleep on it in their one room, but lock-up sheds and stabling for donkeys and ponies would obviate all the evils of the present system. The men are quite willing to pay for a little extra accommodation, and the removal of the mischief which comes of whole areas polluted with decaying vegetable matter is at least worth an experiment.

The density of the population in certain districts, and the sanitary defects of the tenements, are at present absolute dangers to the Public Health. On this ground alone it is desirable to agitate for reform; but there is a broader. ground still - humanity. It is on that broad ground - I venture to ask those who by these scant sketches of a great evil have become in some slight way acquainted with it, to raise their voices and give strength to the cry which is going up at last for a rigid and searching inquiry into the conditions under which the Poor of this vast city live.

To leave the world a little better than he found it, is the best aim a man can have in life, and no labour earns so sweet and so lasting a reward as that which has for its object the happiness of others.

Public opinion boldly expressed never fails to compel the obedience of those who guide the destinies of states. Public opinion is a chorus of voices, and the strength of that chorus depends upon the manner in which each individual member of it exerts his vocal power. How long the scandal which disgraces the age shall continue depends greatly, therefore, good reader, upon your individual exertions. If aught that has been written or drawn here, then, has enlisted your sympathy, pass from a recruit to a good soldier of the cause, and help with all your will and all your strength to make so sad a story as this impossible when in future years abler pen - and pencil than ours shall perhaps once again attempt to tell you-

"HOW THE POOR LIVE."

Lightning Source UK Ltd.
Milton Keynes UK
21 September 2009

143983UK00001B/247/P